FRIENDSHIP

BITE SIZED BIBLE STUDIES

The Friends God Sends

*God's Word On
Friendship & Chick Chat*

6 SESSIONS

BETH JONES

When your words came, I ate them;
they were my joy and my heart's delight . . .
Jeremiah 15:16 NIV

The Bite Sized Bible Study Series Includes . . .

- Satisfied Lives For Desperate Housewives: God's Word On Proverbs 31
- Kissed or Dissed: God's Word For Feeling Rejected & Overlooked
- Grace For The Pace: God's Word For Stressed & Overloaded Lives
- Don't Factor Fear Here: God's Word For Overcoming Anxiety, Fear & Phobias
- The Friends God Sends: God's Word On Friendship & Chick Chat
- What To Do When You Feel Blue: God's Word For Depression & Discouragement

Beth Jones is a Bible teacher, author, wife and mother of four children who ministers the Word of God in a relevant and inspiring way by sharing down-to-earth insights. She is the author of the popular Bible study series Getting A Grip On The Basics which is being used by thousands of churches in America and abroad, the book *Why The Gory, Bloody Details?*, and the Bite Sized Bible Study Series. Beth also writes a bi-weekly newspaper column titled "Just Us Girls" and hosts www.bethjones.org. She and her husband Jeff founded and serve as the senior pastors of Kalamazoo Valley Family Church.

Beth Jones may be reached @
Kalamazoo Valley Family Church, 269.324.5599
www.bethjones.org or www.kvfc.org

FRIENDSHIP

BITE SIZED BIBLE STUDIES

The Friends God Sends

*God's Word On
Friendship & Chick Chat*

6 SESSIONS

BETH JONES

VALLEY PRESS
PUBLISHERS

Valley Press Publishers
Portage, MI

valleypresspublishers.com

The Friends God Sends
God's Word On Friendship & Chick Chat
ISBN: 1-933433-05-1

Published by Valley Press Publishers - A Ministry of KVFC
995 Romence Road, Portage, MI 49024
800-596-0379   www.kvfc.org

Printed in the United States of America.

For information: Please contact Valley Press Publishers.

Contents

The 5 Love Languages

Acknowledgments

Writing a book is like having a baby! I've been "pregnant" with many books over the years and have found that once a book is "conceived" by the Holy Spirit and begins to grow, the gestation period can range from a few years to several decades. Then it seems that at the right time, when I'm "full-term" and "great with child", the Lord puts an "urge" to write within me which eventually triggers the labor pains, transition and ultimately the birth of a book! It takes a lot of people to give birth to a book and I'd like to honor those the Lord has put in my life to coach, pray, support and encourage me in these writing endeavors.

First, my husband, Jeff. You have been my best friend and most consistent encourager. When I have been uncertain, you've always been rock solid and gone the extra mile to help me fulfill God's will in writing. Thanks for loving me and believing in God's call on my life.

Second, my children, Meghan, Annie, Luke and Eric. I've had to take more time away to write; thanks for being understanding and willing to let mom go. I couldn't have asked for four better children. I love you all.

Third, my mom. What an inspiration you have always been to me! Thanks for letting me hang out with you in Florida to write these books.

Fourth, our staff. Our Associate Publisher, April Wedel, our Editorial Coordinator, Juli DeGraaf and our Publications Coordinator, Joanne Davis. I appreciate your love, faith, heart to get the Word out and the long hours you have spent helping me give birth to this book! I also want to thank the entire KVFC staff for their love, support and encouragement.

Fifth, all the volunteer copy editors and pray-ers. A very special thanks to Mary VanderWal, Carol Lacey and Elise Burch for your time, comments and editing help. I especially appreciate my dear praying friends Mary VanderWal, Mary Jo Fox, Kate Cook, Cindy Boester, Jennifer Nederhoed, Pam Roe-Vanderberg, Jennifer Palthe, Colleen DeBruin, Molly Nicolai, KVFC prayer teams and many others who have continually lifted me and these projects to the Lord in prayer.

Sixth, Pat Judd, Bryan Norris and all the guys with CrossStaff. Thanks for partnering with us in this project. Let's have fun watching what the Lord will do!

I love God's Word. I don't just like it; I love it. It's more valuable to me than anything. If I had to spend the rest of my life on a remote, uninhabited island and could only take one thing, I would take my Bible. Why? It's simple. God has changed and upgraded every area of my life as I have simply read, believed and obeyed the Bible.

It wasn't always that way. Like many people, I had never even considered reading the Bible for myself, much less studying it. The Bible was for priests, theologians and monks. It was not relevant to my life. It was a dusty old book in our basement. One day, when I was about 14 years old, I just got the "urge" to read the Bible. I started with Genesis, and within the first few chapters I fell asleep. That was the end of my Bible reading.

It wasn't until five years later when I was a 19-year-old college freshman that my roommate began to share with me what the Bible said about God, about life and about me. I was shocked at the "living" quality of the Bible. It wasn't like any other book I read. This wasn't like reading the president's biography. This wasn't like reading the dull Western Civilization textbooks in front of me. It was as if God Himself was explaining the contents to me. Something was happening in my heart as I read God's Word. I was challenged. I was encouraged. I was comforted. The Living God was speaking through His Living Word. During this time I developed a hunger for God and His Word. I stayed up late to read the Bible. I pondered it during the day. There was plenty I didn't understand, but I received strength, energy and wisdom just by reading it, and ultimately the Holy Spirit drew me to Jesus.

As a new Christian in my sophomore year of college, my Bible study leader simply exhorted me to read my Bible a lot and "let the Word of Christ dwell richly inside of me." It was the best advice ever! The result was that I began to develop an insatiable appetite for God's Word and a passionate desire to share God's Word with others. As I read my Bible, Jesus walked off the pages and came to live in my heart. Jesus isn't just alive in heaven, He is alive to me. I've come to know Him intimately through fellowship with Him in His Word.

Isn't it great that God's Word is interactive—not just historic or static? God's Word is living and active and able to effectually work within us to affect change and impart the miraculous! The Bible is the most amazing book ever! It has been banned, burned and blasted, but it lives on and continues to be the world's best-selling book.

Unfortunately, I have found that lots of people just don't understand the Bible and as a result, they get overwhelmed, bored or frustrated. Many Christians have never really tasted the rich, daily, life-changing flavor of God's Word. If you want to grow and mature in God, you have to "eat" large quantities of the Word. Once you taste and see that the Lord and His Word are good, nothing else will satisfy you! Think of it this way: if all you've ever tasted are peanut butter and jelly sandwiches, then you are pretty content with a good PBJ. But the minute you taste a filet mignon, you can never again be satisfied by a PBJ. In some ways, I have found that is the story for many Christians. If you're one of those people that have been content with a spiritual PBJ, I've got good news for you; get your taste buds ready for some rich, tasty, "meaty" morsels from God's Word. The more you eat it, the better it tastes!

Our goal in the Bite Sized Bible Study Series is to create an addiction in you for Bible study, and more importantly for knowing God intimately through the revelation knowledge of His Word, by His Spirit. As you explore these studies, I believe that the Holy Spirit will speak to your heart and transmit the supernatural revelation you need to operate victoriously in this life.

Jeremiah was right:

"When your words came, I ate them;
they were my joy and my heart's delight . . ."
Jeremiah 15:16, NIV

May this be your testimony, too!

This Bible study can be used individually as well as in small groups. It's ideal for those who are hungry to learn from the Word, but who have a limited amount of time to meet together with others.

The Bite Sized Bible Study Series is designed for all types of Bible study formats.

- Individual Study
- Women's Small Groups
- Lunchtime Study at Work
- Neighborhood Bible Study
- Couples' Small Groups
- Sunday School Class
- Prison Ministry
- Student and Youth Small Groups
- Outreach Bible Study
- Early Morning Men's Bible Groups
- Singles Small Groups
- Recovery and Felt Need Groups

For Individual Study

Pray. Ask God, by the Holy Spirit, to customize these sessions for you personally.

Expect. Turn your "expectation" on and trust God to speak to your heart.

Dive. Grab your Bible, pen and favorite beverage and dive in!

For Small Group Study Leaders

Pray. Ask God, by the Holy Spirit, to reveal and customize these sessions for you and your group members.

Expect. Turn your "expectation" on and trust God to speak to your heart, as well as the hearts of those in your small group.

Facilitate. Small groups will do better with a facilitator, preferably a more mature Christian who can add helpful comments as well as lead a heartfelt time of prayer before and after each session. It's important that you keep things moving in the right direction. As the leader of the small group, keep in mind that it's your job to facilitate discussion and not act as the "teacher" who does all the talking. It's important for those in the group to verbalize their discoveries, so do your best to create an atmosphere where each member feels free to share what they are learning from God's Word.

Encourage. Encourage everyone to participate. Help those who talk a lot to take a breather and let others share their insights as well.

Focus. Stay focused on God the Father, Jesus, and the Holy Spirit Who gave us the Scriptures. Our goal is to see what God has said in His Word. Keep in mind that this is a Bible study and not a place for "my opinion" or "my church believes" or "here's what I think" comments. Always direct people's attention back to the Bible to see what the Scriptures say.

Highlight. Hit the high points. If you face time constraints, you may not have enough time to cover every detail of each lesson. As the leader, prayerfully prepare and be sure you cover the highlights of each session.

Digest. We've endeavored to "cut up" the Word through this Bite Sized Bible Study, and as a leader it's your job to help those in your small group digest the Scriptures so they can benefit from all the spiritual nutrition in each word.

Discuss. Take time to answer the three discussion questions at the end of each Bible study session. These should help stimulate heartfelt conversation.

First Things First

If you want this Bible study to really impact your life, you must be certain of one major thing: you must be certain you are a Christian according to God's definition and instruction in the Bible. You must be certain that you are accepted by God; that you are saved. So let's begin our study by considering this important issue.

Did you know that some people want to be a Christian on their terms, rather than on God's terms? Sometimes people want to emphasize church, religion and their goodness as evidence of their Christianity. For some, it will be a rude awakening to discover that the Bible tells us God isn't impressed by any of those substitutes. Did you know that God isn't interested in our denominational tags? He's not wowed by our church membership pedigree, either. He's not moved by our good deeds and benevolent accomplishments. The thing that most impresses God is His Son, Jesus Christ. *"For God so loved the world that he gave his one and only Son, that whoever believes in him shall not perish but have eternal life." John 3:16, NIV* God paid quite a price to send His own Son to the cross to pay the penalty for our sin. It's really an insult to Him to trust in or substitute anything or anyone else for Jesus Christ. The key to being a Christian is to believe in, trust, receive and confess Jesus Christ as your Lord and Savior.

Why would you or anyone want to believe in, trust, receive and confess Jesus Christ as Lord? Why would you want to know Jesus personally and to be known by Him? Unless you truly understand your condition before God, you wouldn't have any reason to! However, when you realize the magnitude of your sin—those private and public thoughts, deeds, actions and words that you and God know about—when you listen to your conscience and realize that truly "all have sinned," including you, it can be very sobering. It's even more sobering to realize that according to God's justice system, *". . . the wages of sin is death . . ." Romans 6:23 NKJV* It's a big wake up call when it really hits you that the consequence of sin is death. Death which is defined as an eternal separation from God is the payment you will receive for your sin. When you realize your true, hopeless, lost condition before God, you will run to Him in order to be saved. This reality causes people to quit playing religious games and to quit trusting in their own works of righteousness. Our lost condition forces us to forgo being "churchy" or "religious", apathetic, passive and indifferent, and to become hungry for the Merciful Living God. It's good news to discover that " . . . *the gift of God is eternal life in Christ Jesus our Lord." Romans 6:23 NKJV*

What does God require of us? The qualification for eternal life is simply to believe on Jesus. Many people say they believe in God or in Jesus Christ. In fact, the Bible tells us that the devil himself believes and trembles. According to the Bible, God's definition of a Christian believer—or a Christ One—is the person who believes in their heart that God raised Jesus from the dead and who confesses with his or her mouth that Jesus Christ is their Lord. In other words, their heart and mouth agree that Jesus is Lord! We see this in Romans 10:13, 9, ". . . *whoever calls on the name of the LORD shall be saved . . . if you confess with your mouth the Lord Jesus and believe in your heart that God has raised Him from the dead, you will be saved." NKJV*

This is something we do on purpose. It's a sobering thought to consider that if you've never purposely repented of your sin and invited Jesus Christ to be the Lord of your life, you may not be saved—you may not be a Christian according to God's definition. Would you like to be certain that you are a Christian; that you have a relationship with the Lord and eternal salvation? It's simple, just answer these questions: Do you believe that God raised Jesus from the dead? Will you give Him the steering wheel of your life and trust Him to forgive all your sins and make you an entirely new person? Will you trust Jesus Christ alone to save you? Are you willing to invite Him into your life and will you confess that He is your Lord? If so, please pray this prayer from your heart. God will hear you, Jesus Christ will forgive your sins and enter your life. You will be a Christian.

"Dear God, I come to you as a person who recognizes my condition before you. I see that I am a sinner in need of a Savior. Jesus, I do believe that God raised You from the dead and I now invite you into my life. I confess Jesus as my Lord. I want to know You and be the Christian You have called me to be, according to Your definition. I thank You, in Jesus' Name. Amen."

Relationships. People. Girlfriendships. Remember these friendships? Lucille Ball and Ethel Mertz. Betty and Veronica. Mary Ann and Ginger. (Were they friends?) Wilma and Betty. Rachel, Monica and Phoebe. Oprah and Gayle. Ruth and Naomi. Mary and Elizabeth.

Girls and friendship are like peanut butter and jelly; they just go together! *"Make new friends but keep the old, one is silver and the other's gold."* We sang it in Girl Scouts; little did we know how true those words were. There's oxygen and there's friendship!

Bette Midler and Barry Manilow both told us, *"You've got to have frieeeends!"* Carole King promised, *"Lean on me when you're not strong and I'll be your friend, I'll help you carry on . . ."* *"Just look over your shoulder honey, I'll be there . . ."* thank you Jackson Five! Carly Simon and James Taylor told us, *"Winter, spring, summer or fall all you have to do is call and I'll be there, yes I will, you've got a friend."* Michael W. Smith reminded us, *"Friends are friends forever when the Lord's the Lord of them . . ."* Barbara Streisand summed it up, *"People who need people are the luckiest people . . ."* Are you one of those lucky people? Is friendship something you crave and cultivate?

What would Panera's, Starbucks or a shopping trip be like without a chick friend? How do you survive a carpooling crisis without a friend? Who do you call when you need prayer? Who do you share your extra 10,000 words a day with? Without girlfriends, life would be so . . . so . . . so full

Be careful the environment you choose for it will shape you; be careful the friends you choose for you will become like them

W. Clement Stone

of testosterone! We love our men, but boys are not girls. As one person said, "Girls talk, therefore we are friends."

You probably received this forwarded e-mail several times, just like I did. Although we don't know who the author is, this certainly sums up friendship among women.

> *Time passes.*
> *Life happens.*
> *Distance separates.*
> *Children grow up.*
> *Love waxes and wanes.*
> *Hearts break.*
> *Careers end.*
> *Jobs come and go.*
> *Parents die.*
> *Colleagues forget favors.*
> *Men don't call when they say they will.*
> *Girlfriends are there,*
> *no matter how much time and how many miles are between you.*
> *A girlfriend is never farther away than needing her can reach.*

How I Learned This Lesson

As long as I can remember, my life has been filled with "girl friendships." It's been said that some friendships are for a reason, or a season or a lifetime. Here's my story. It started with my mother, who has been a friend and confidant for the largest chunk of my life. Her sense of humor, positive outlook on life and "can do" attitude made her fun to be around. I'm the oldest of four girls, so my three sisters and I have always been friends. Although we fought like sisters can in our teen years, we have always been close and kindred. In our early teens my dad left my mother and after their divorce, ours was an estrogen-filled chick house! We learned how to talk, listen, cry, laugh, fight, forgive, push hormonal buttons, steal each other's clothing, tampons, earrings and love each other through thick and thin.

Andi and Laurie are the first "non-sister" girlfriends I remember. I was the new student at Winans Elementary, and my biggest fear as a third grader was that I wouldn't make any new friends. Andi and Laurie lived in my neighborhood and we were all in Miss Earhart's class. When they invited me to their Brownie troop, I knew I was in the group! What began in third grade continued through high school and college, and turned out to be a real divine connection, a God-knit friendship!

In junior high and high school the gang grew. Chick friends roll call - Tammy, Mary Jane, Kim, Jennifer, Diane, Carol, Lisa, Deedee, Heather, Sara, Sheila, Anne and Stacey. *(Not their real names!)* Thirteen girls plus me made up "our group." We have history—Girl Scout camp, boy crushes, toilet papering neighborhoods, sleepovers, supposed séances where we tried to revive Abraham Lincoln from the dead and asked him to blow out the candle in the room, stealing cigs from our parents, getting drunk at lunch and high on the weekends, being mall rats, making fake IDs, playing sports, running student council and somehow getting good grades. We bonded. I hate to tell you, but we were the kids every Christian parent hopes their children don't hang out with!

It's a long story, but at the end of our senior year of high school, Andi had a life-changing encounter with Jesus as her personal Lord and Savior: it was dramatic. Our whole "group" thought she had flipped. Andi and I roomed together our freshman year in college, and although I was the "fish" that fought all the way to the boat, it was Andi that led me to the Lord. Somewhere during the past few decades several of us in "the group" have had definite, supernatural experiences with the Lord and Jesus has taken center stage of some of our lives. As we approach our 30th class reunion, although it's a bit harder with everyone's busy life, we still try to get together once a year between Christmas and New Year. We rehash the old days, we notice a few more wrinkles and we are thankful for the season of friendship we've had.

Into college and young adult life, Michelle and Mary Jo were my bosom buddies and confidants. As a born-again Christian, friendships took on a whole new dimension. Jesus was the glue in all of our friendships—we shared, laughed, grew in our faith and prayed about the good, the bad and the ugly. Michelle was my first "Jonathan-David" friend (more on that in later), and when she moved to

Florida after college, the Lord brought Mary Jo into my life for another rich "Jonathan-David" friendship season.

You know how it goes. We all got married; started families and the pace took off! Friendships went to the back burner, the letters and phone calls were more spaced out (this was before e-mail!), and girl-times became a sweet memory.

My husband, Jeff, and I enjoyed our new married life being best friends with one another; we did everything together. We had four babies in six years, pioneered and pastored a growing church and life was busy, busy, busy. My girl friendships were nil.

One day, 13 years into my marriage, although I loved my husband dearly, I was longing for a friend to just go do "girl stuff" with. It was during this time that I had a major revelation—I had sown a friendship famine! What I mean is this: I had not planted any real lasting friendship seeds, I had not invested my heart in any new personal friends and the result was that I didn't have any! Yes, I had lots of acquaintances and since we were pastoring a church, there were lots of wonderful Christian girls who had become casual friends in my world, but I had not really connected with any long-term heart friends.

ঌ**Nugget**ঌ It's interesting, but for those of you in certain professions or circumstances in life—those in ministry, pastoral work, teachers, doctors, influential women or the wife of an influential man and so on—often it's difficult to find the balance between "professional relationships" and "friendships." Sometimes the nature of our work or lot in life makes it awkward and difficult to determine the genuine nature or motives of those seeking our company. It was true for me; I found that it was sometimes difficult to find a friend. Because of the various hats I wore, it could sometimes be confusing to be friends with gals in the church since on one hand I was a pastor and spiritual leader/mentor to them, and on the other hand I was the "let your hair down" friend. Often, it's not possible to be both. If you are a pastor's wife in particular, you know how tough this can be. It's easy to begin to feel like you are on your own lonely little island.

In the early years of our growing church, Tara was a friend that I could share my heart with. We had been casual friends in Bible school and although she and her husband were on staff at our church, we found a way to make it work and cultivated a dear friendship. Her heart for God and sense of humor were refreshing.

At the same time, I continued praying for another "Jonathan-David" friendship; I missed this type of friend. The pace of pastoring a growing church and raising four kids was sometimes overwhelming and I just wanted a girl friend. I remember writing an advertisement that I never posted.

"Married, pastor's wife and Bible teacher, looking for a best friend. Must love God and be sold out for Him. Must enjoy drinking cappuccinos and cheering for your kids, like a wild woman, at soccer and basketball games. Sense of humor a must. To inquire, meet me at Starbucks."

The Lord answered my prayer. It wasn't long before He brought Mary into my life, and we've been like two peas in a pod for the past five years. We've yakked for hours, prayed for hours, cried for hours. We've been known to e-mail, instant message and call each other on the phone within a fifteen-minute span, and if we're lucky we'll be meeting for a cappie (i.e. cappuccino) within the hour! Our husbands find it amusing. Her friendship has been an answer to prayer; a God-knit friendship. I believe God wants to give us those special heart-friends, like Jonathan and David enjoyed. Later, we'll spend an entire chapter talking about that subject.

A real friend is one who walks in when the rest of the world walks out. Walter Winchell

Jesus had the *multitudes*, the *twelve*, the *three* and the *one* . . . and in my own life I have seen a similar pattern in the friends' arena. My girl friend famine has been replaced with a girl friend garden. When it rains it pours. Today, I can say that the Lord has put a wonderful group of girls into my life on a daily basis: God-knit heart friends, prayer partners, the sold-out girls on our staff; the growing group of hip, relevant, fun, God-loving women in our church; ministry friends around the world; and to top it off, I've got a group of fun neighborhood friends.

How's your friendship world? Why don't you take a sentimental journey and recount the women—the multitudes, the twelve, the three and the one—the Lord has brought in and out of your life? See if you can identify any healthy or unhealthy relational patterns. Get an honest read on your current friendship status, and then believe God that as you study this subject He will give you the wisdom you need to cultivate and sow into the rich friendships He wants for your life.

Friendship Realities

The first thing God said about relationships in the Bible makes it plain! *"It is not good that man should be alone."* It is not good to be lonely. It is not good to be friendless. It is not good to continually fail at relationships.

God wants your relationships to be blessed! Talking, walking, eating, hanging out, playing, praying, working, fighting and serving—the Bible is full of heartfelt, complex, personal and dynamic relationships! God is into people. He is relational. He has created us with a great capacity for friends; for giving and receiving His love to and through others.

Unfortunately, many people—believers and unbelievers alike—are alone! Many people are lonely. They do not have a heart connection with others. Relationship experts tell us that millions of people in America have never had one minute where they could let down and share their deepest feelings with another person. What about you? Are you one of those people? Are you fulfilled and satisfied in your relationships? Is your heart empty? Lonely? Alone? Is it time to believe God for some friends? Is it time to ask God to blow fresh wind into the sails of your existing friendships?

The Ten Most Wanted Friends

Jesus is our best friend that sticks closer than a brother, He's our first love, but because He knows the value of godly relationships, He brings us together with His family in such a way that He provides divine, God-breathed, God-ordained, God-knit friendships.

God's Word is loaded with wisdom on friendship. He tells us what kind of friend we should be, what type of friends to avoid and how to be a better friend. In their book, *"Dealing With People You Can't Stand"*, authors Dr. Rick Brinkman and Dr. Rick Kirschner identify the *"Ten Most Unwanted"* personality types.[1] These are the people you want to avoid and the person you don't want to be. Let's turn that around and see the *"Ten Most Wanted"* personality types according to God's Word.

#1. Miss Aromatherapy: — *to Enjoy*
 Friends That Refresh Our Soul

Candles, lotions, oils, soap, incense and bath beads—you name a scent and you can get it. My favorite year round soothing, refreshing scent is sandalwood. I like most spice and flower scents, but I can't do food-scented things. Give me a tulip tart or patchouli-scented oil, and although I'll have flashbacks to Spencer Gifts in 1975, I'm happy. But light a cookiedough-scented candle and I'm gagging. Each of us favors particular refreshing scents. It's true in friendship, too.

As Christians, we carry the sweet aroma of Christ. *"But thanks be to God! For through what Christ has done, he has triumphed over us so that now wherever we go he uses us to tell others about the Lord and to spread the Gospel like a sweet perfume. 15 As far as God is concerned there is a sweet, wholesome fragrance in our lives. It is the fragrance of Christ within us, an aroma to both the saved and the unsaved all around us. 16 To those who are not being saved, we seem a fearful smell of death and doom, while to those who know Christ we are a life-giving perfume."* 2 Corinthians 2:14-16, TLB Let's look at the fragrance of friendship that refreshes us.

1.   Proverbs 27:9

        Underline the phrase "sweet friendship."

        Just as lotions and fragrance give sensual delight, a sweet friendship refreshes the soul. The Message

Why do you think that lotions and fragrances are compared to a sweet friendship?

_____

Describe a friend in your life and the type of aroma they give off. _____

_____

2.   Proverbs 25:13

Underline the phrase "reliable friends."

"Reliable friends who do what they say are like cool drinks in sweltering heat — refreshing!" The Message

What type of friend refreshes us? _____

Describe what makes a reliable friend refreshing. _____

3.   1 Corinthians 16:17-18, 2 Corinthians 7:13

In these passages, underline the blessings we receive (or give) as friends.

17 I was glad when Stephanas, Fortunatus and Achaicus arrived, because they have supplied what was lacking from you. 18 For they refreshed my spirit and yours also. Such men deserve recognition.
1 Corinthians 16:17-18, NIV

13 By all this we are encouraged. In addition to our own encouragement, we were especially delighted to see how happy Titus was, because his spirit has been refreshed by all of you.
2 Corinthians 7:13-14, NIV

What does getting together with godly friends do for your spirit?

_____

Describe your get togethers with girl friends; what type of things do you like to do?

_____

_____

4.   Philemon 7

Underline the words that describe the encouragement Paul received from his Christian friends.

For I have derived great joy and comfort and encouragement from your love, because the hearts of the saints [who are your fellow Christians] have been cheered and refreshed through you, [my] brother. AMP

A godly friend is a gift.

According to this passage, what does a good friend add to our lives?

_____

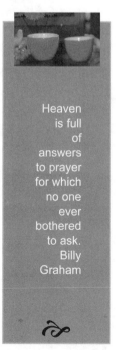

Heaven is full of answers to prayer for which no one ever bothered to ask.
Billy Graham

#2.   Miss Lip Balm: Friends That Pray

The thing I value most in a friend is their heart to pray. I love friends that talk, giggle, shop and hang out with me, but the thing I most treasure is a friend that prays! A praying friend knows God. One of the my favorite things to do is to pray with friends! It's so nice to have friends that enjoy praying together—to pray for each other, our husbands, our children, our church, our community, our country and our world . . . whatever the Holy Spirit prompts us to pray about! A group of us moms—Karen, Pam, Mary and I—have been praying together for our children for several years. Those prayer sessions have been a great place to share laughter, tears, advice and heartfelt prayer. To have a praying friend and to be a praying friend is a treasure. When you have a friend that knows how to make real contact with God and pray effectual prayers that heaven answers, you are blessed. If you *are* that type of friend, you are a major blessing!

1.   Romans 15:32

Underline the thing that results when we have God-ordained relationships.

30 Will you be my prayer partners? For the Lord Jesus Christ's sake and because of your love for me-given to you by the Holy Spirit-pray much with me for my work. 31 Pray that I will be protected in Jerusalem from those who are not Christians. Pray also that the Christians there will be willing to accept the money I am bringing them. 32 Then I will be able to come to you with a happy heart by the will of God, and we can refresh each other. TLB

What did Paul need from his friends? _____

What types of prayers did Paul request? _____

What did Paul say would happen for him and his friends when, by God's will, they were united?

_____

2.   Job 42:10

Underline the phrase "prayed for his friends."

After Job had prayed for his friends, the LORD made him prosperous again and gave him twice as much as he had before. NIV

Job's friends had not been that good to Job. Nevertheless, what did Job do for his friends?

_____

What did God end up doing for Job? _____

If you're looking for help in praying prayers that God will answer, why not pray the prayers that the Holy Spirit inspired Paul to pray for his Christian friends? Just insert your friend's name into these prayers. (If you want to super-size this prayer, I encourage you to read it from the Amplified Bible as well.)

I pray for you (insert your friend's name here) constantly, asking God, the glorious Father of our Lord Jesus Christ, to give you wisdom to see clearly and really understand who Christ is and all that he has done for you. I pray that your hearts will be flooded with light so that you can see something of the future he has called you to share. I want you to realize that God has been made rich because we who are Christ's have been given to him! I pray that you will begin to understand how incredibly great his power is to help those who believe him. Ephesians 1:15-19, TLB

And I pray that Christ will be more and more at home in your hearts (insert your friends name here), living within you as you trust in him. May your roots go down deep into the soil of God's marvelous love; and may you be able to feel and understand, as all God's children should, how long, how wide, how deep, and how high his love really is; and to experience this love for yourselves, though it is so great that you will never see the end of it or fully know or understand it. And so at last you will be filled up with God himself. Ephesians 3:17-18, TLB

. . . we have kept on praying and asking God to help you (insert your friends name here) understand what he wants you to do; asking him to make you wise about spiritual things; and asking that the way you live will always please the Lord and honor him, so that you will always be doing good, kind things for others, while all the time you are learning to know God better and better. We are praying, too, that you will be filled with his mighty, glorious strength so that you can keep going no matter what happens-always full of the joy of the Lord, and always thankful to the Father who has made us fit to share all the wonderful things that belong to those who live in the Kingdom of light. Colossians 1:9-13, TLB

#3.   Miss Perfect Bra: Friends That Lift You Up

Ever felt like a Martian in Victoria's Secret? Whose body do they make that stuff for? I would not look sexy in most of those things; I'd look like an injured Shamu! We sounded like a bunch of giggling high school girls a few years ago. Several of us had a girl's day out and we took over the fitting rooms of the lingerie department at the local department store to try on the new "water bra." Some of us saw cleavage for the first time— ours! It was fun to dream. There is something about finding the right bra; the straps stay in place, it shapes us perfectly and gives us the needed lift. We need the kind of friends who will lift us up!

John Maxwell describes twenty-five "People Principles" in his book, *Winning With People*.[2] He identifies being the kind of friend that lifts people up, what he calls the Elevator Principle, as one huge key to great relationships. Joyce Landorf Heatherly, author of *Balcony People*[3] describes the difference between balcony and basement friends. Let's see what the Bible says about friends that lift us up.

1.   Exodus 17:12

Underline the key word that describes Aaron and Hur's help for Moses.

But Moses' hands became heavy; so they took a stone and put it under him, and he sat on it. And Aaron and Hur supported his hands, one on one side, and the other on the other side; and his hands were steady until the going down of the sun. NKJV

What role did Aaron and Hur play in helping Moses get the victory? _____

_____

In times of stress, pressure, deadlines, fast-pace, turmoil or emergency, do you have a support system in your life?

_____

List those who are in your support system: _____

_____

Are you the type of person that lifts up those around you? _____

2.   Proverbs 12:25

Underline one of the causes of depression and one of the causes of gladness.

An anxious heart weighs a man down, but a kind word cheers him up. NIV

What does a good word do for us? _____

_____

Describe a recent experience you've had in hearing a kind word.

_____

If you want to lift yourself up, lift up someone else. Booker T. Washington

Who gave you your last good word? _____

3.   Ephesians 4:29

Underline the phrase "building others up."

Do not let any unwholesome talk come out of your mouths, but only what is helpful for building others up according to their needs, that it may benefit those who listen. NIV

What type of words should we avoid? _____

What type of words should we speak? _____

What do good words do for people? _____

#4.   Miss Chocolate Cake: Friends That Comfort

Are you a chocoholic? Are there times of the month where you would walk 5 miles, in snow, up hill, both ways to get chocolate? *(Wait, isn't that what your parents did to get to school?)* I know lots of women who crave chocolate. It's a comfort food. There are many times in our lives that we just need some comfort—someone to understand, empathize, encourage and comfort.

1.   Job 2:11-12

Underline the phrase "Job's three friends."

11 When Job's three friends, Eliphaz the Temanite, Bildad the Shuhite and Zophar the Naamathite, heard about all the troubles that had come upon him, they set out from their homes and met together by agreement to go and sympathize with him and comfort him. NIV

When Job faced a storm, what did his three friends do? _____

_____

As it turned out, these friends didn't provide the comfort and wisdom that Job needed. Initially, their hearts were probably in the right place in that they desired to provide comfort. Unfortunately, they did not follow God's wisdom in providing that comfort.

2.	2 Corinthians 7:6

Underline the things that God did for Paul through his friend, Titus.

But God, Who comforts and encourages and refreshes and cheers the depressed and the sinking, comforted and encouraged and refreshed and cheered us by the arrival of Titus. AMP

What did the arrival of Paul's friend Titus do for Paul? _____

It's amazing how the right person at the right time can be used of God to comfort, encourage, refresh and cheer us up.

Who has encouraged you lately? _____

Who have you encouraged lately? _____

## #5.	Miss Double Shot Espresso: Friends That Celebrate

Espresso, cappuccino, mochas and lattes all have the capacity to charge your life with a celebrated burst of energy. If you need an afternoon jolt, what do you drink? Years ago some of our relatives came to visit our church. They were from a more conservative church background and our style of worship was new and different for them. After church we asked them how they liked the service. Their comment made us laugh. They said they loved the enthusiastic celebration of worship and described us as *"the church on caffeine!"* We took that as a compliment. We need those espresso-filled friends in our lives—the energetic, upbeat, positive, motivators—those that will celebrate with us!

It's not always easy to find these types of friends—those who are genuinely happy for your success. Jealousy, envy and competition often enter friendship among women. It doesn't have to be that way. Who in your life is the "shot in the arm" friend; the one that motivates and celebrates with you? Are you that type of friend?

1.   Song of Solomon 5:1

Underline the phrase "Celebrate with me, friends!"

Celebrate with me, friends! Raise your glasses — "To life! To love!"
The Message

What do we need to do for our friends? _____

The lover in Song of Solomon wanted her friends to share her joy. It's great to rejoice when good fortune and God's blessings are overflowing in the lives of your friends.

⮞**Nugget**⮜ Early in my Christian life, I remember feeling left out, jealous and envious of God's blessings in my friend's lives. That was a sign of my immaturity. All of us have to grow in faith and in God's love so that we eliminate jealousy and envy from our lives and we rejoice with those who rejoice! There are times when your friend is celebrating her greatest moments, while you may be facing your most difficult moments. A friend with strong character and an unselfish heart will be able to rejoice in the success and blessing of God in someone else's life, even if their own life does not seem so blessed at the moment. That's when we have to guard against jealousy and envy.

Oprah Winfrey and Gayle King are best friends. Oprah tells the story of a defining moment in their friendship. *"When you are in the public eye, you need a friend you can trust."* That trust doesn't come easily to someone like Oprah. She's found that friend in Gayle. Oprah says, *"Gayle genuinely – and I could cry when I say this – I have never met a human being more genuinely excited about my success than she is. There has never been one moment of jealousy. I don't know – if our roles were reversed—if I could have given my entire open heart to someone I saw whose career was blasting off from the earth, and say, 'You go, girl, go to the moon.' I don't know if I could do that."[4]*

Describe a time in your life when you overcame the temptation to be jealous or envious of God's blessings in a friend's life.

_____

_____

2.   Proverbs 14:10

Underline the phrase "bitter moments" and the word "celebrations."

The person who shuns the bitter moments of friends will be an outsider at their celebrations.
The Message

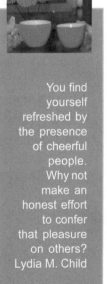

We need to be the type of friend that is there in the tough times and during the celebrations. We can't just be the "happy" friend; we need to be there with a shoulder to cry on during the tough times, as well.

What does this verse tell us about friendship in bitter moments?

_____

You find yourself refreshed by the presence of cheerful people. Why not make an honest effort to confer that pleasure on others? Lydia M. Child

What does this verse tell us about friendship in celebrations?

#6. Miss Double-Dip In A Waffle Cone: Friends That Are Generous

When the ice cream clerk asks our kids if they want their ice cream in a cup, cone or waffle cone, they turn around and look at us with that *"pleeeeeeeease, can I have a waffle cone"* look!

My sisters and I grew up shopping on the clearance rack! Today my mother is very generous, but when we were growing up she was very frugal. As a single mom raising me and my three sisters, money was tight so she taught us how to shop the discounted, marked down, "all sales final" rack. We knew how to find the deals! Once my mother was asked, *"Have you ever purchased anything that wasn't on clearance?"* Her response was, *"Dear me, I hope not!"* She was serious. I remember going grocery shopping as a teen and loading the cart with generic brand groceries. It didn't occur to me to look for anything else; mother had taught me well! I thought you were a rich kid if your family ate Delmonte brand fruits and vegetables! Welcome to my world! I had developed a "poverty" mentality.

When I got married, that changed! My husband is a very generous person, and soon after we were married he helped me break out of the "clearance" mentality. I'll never forget the day he took me shopping and made me pay full price for several new outfits. He would not let me buy anything on sale! It was weird, but wonderful!

We need friends like that in our lives and we need to be that type of friend to others. Generous and giving. Are you a "clearance rack" friend or do you give generously to others?

1.   Proverbs 14:20

Underline the phrase "many friends."

The poor are shunned even by their neighbors, but the rich have many friends. NIV

Who doesn't have friends? _____

Who has many friends? _____

This verse could be describing a negative truth; that because of wrong motives, the rich have lots of friends.

Let's think about this verse from the positive side. Since it's true that you cannot give what you do not have, if you were rich in God, rich in joy, rich in peace, rich in wisdom, rich in wealth—and generous in sharing your riches—would people be attracted to you?

_____

What do you have that you ought to think about giving to others? _____

_____

2.   Proverbs 19:4

Underline the phrase "attracts friends."

Wealth attracts friends as honey draws flies, but poor people are avoided like a plague. The Message

This passage describes the same thing.

What does wealth attract? _____

What does poverty produce? _____

This is interesting, because as believers we are to reach out to poor and rich alike. God loves people of all economic levels. At the same time, if you have wealth, a humble heart and are generous with your wealth, you become an attractive friend.

☙**Nugget**❧ Do you think this passage is talking about "buying" friendship? Is it possible to be "wealthy" in other ways and generous towards your friends and reap real, genuine friendships? In your friendships, are you generous? Are you stingy? Do you always request separate checks when you go to lunch with a friend? Do you offer to buy lunch or mochas? Do you look for ways to give gifts, surprises, notes and other special things to your friends at appropriate and even uneventful times? Be a generous, giving friend!

3.   Isaiah 32:8

Underline the phrases "generous man," "generous things" and "by generosity."

But a generous man devises generous things, and by generosity he shall stand. NKJV

What does a generous person do? _____

What makes a person stand and/or stand out? _____

Have you devised any generous plans lately? Are you on the lookout for ways to be a blessing to your friends? Free yourself from a spirit of stinginess and the next time you go out with your girlfriends, pay the bill and surprise them!

#7. Miss Salt Scrub Exfoliate: Friends That Tell You The Truth

Last Christmas my fourteen-year-old daughter, Annie, said, *"Mom, please don't get me any more lotions, bath gel, body spray or glitter."* She said that for the past decade of her life, she's been given oodles of skin and body products for every birthday and Christmas, and it would take her the rest of her life to use them. I had to laugh, because she was right!

There is a plethora of bath and body stores, spas, lotions, ointments, oils, salt scrubs, masks, peels and every body care product you could want. I especially love the salt scrub exfoliates when my hands and feet are feeling extra dry. It's great for sloughing off gross, dry, dead cells! Do you have people in your life like this?

We need exfoliating friends; people who will challenge us, rub us the wrong way at times and sharpen us! With friends like this, we can be the pure, aromatic and radiant generation of women God has called us to be.

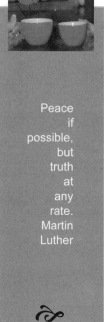

1.   Proverbs 2:16

Underline the phrase "wise friends."

Wise friends will rescue you from the Temptress — that smooth-talking Seductress. The Message

What will a wise and good friend do if they observe you heading down the wrong path?

_____

&Nugget& Don't get mad when your friends tell you the truth. If your girl friend is heading

Peace if possible, but truth at any rate. Martin Luther

towards destruction, it takes courage to tell her the truth. I've heard more than one story of women who dissed their girlfriend who told them the truth about a man they were dating. For some reason, there are women that don't want to know that the man they are dating is a married, cheating, womanizing, snake in the grass. They'd rather go on in their fake bliss and then get mad at the woman who told them the truth. If you observed your friend making choices that were unhealthy or ungodly, would you have the courage to rescue them?

2.   Proverbs 27:6

Underline the phrase "wounds of a friend."

Faithful are the wounds of a friend, but the kisses of an enemy are deceitful. NKJV

People that don't love you can flatter you, compliment you and tell you all the things you want to hear, but in the end what is it?

_____

A true friend tells you the truth, but often what does it feel like? _____

_____

3.   Proverbs 27:17

Underline the phrase "the countenance of his friend."

As iron sharpens iron, so a man sharpens the countenance of his friend. NKJV

When you rub pieces of iron together, sparks fly, friction heats up, but the iron is sharpened.

How do friends sharpen each other? _____

How do you handle conflict and disagreement? _____

_____

In friendship, sometimes there is conflict and disagreement as well as encouragement and accountability.

What does it mean to be accountable to your friends? _____

When a friend sharpens you, they help your life become more congruent to God's Word and His will, and the result is a peace and purity that changes your very countenance.

#8. Miss Cosmetic Bag: Friends That Cover And Forgive

What's in your make up bag? Miracle working power, right? Our foundation, blush, cover up, lipstick, eye shadow, mascara all serve one purpose—to cover up our imperfections and make us look beautiful. We need friends like that.

1. Proverbs 17:9

Underline the phrase "close friends."

He who covers over an offense promotes love, but whoever repeats the matter separates close friends. NIV

I love how The Message Bible translates this verse.

Overlook an offense and bond a friendship; fasten on to a slight and — good-bye, friend! The Message

If you choose to cover and forgive the sins, offenses and missteps of your friend, what are you promoting?

_____

How do you cover an offense? _____

All of us make mistakes. We say the wrong thing, we do the wrong thing, we let our flesh dominate us at times, and it's nice to know we have friends who won't hold our mistakes over our head and they won't blab our faults to others.

&**Nugget**&- This is an interesting concept. Many people feel obligated to expose and shame someone who has made a mistake or offense. There is a certain sense of self-righteousness that goes along with pointing out other people's flaws. Jesus told us the qualifications for "throwing stones." He said if we haven't sinned then we can throw the first stone. The flesh will want to accuse, suspect, expose and broadcast another person's faults and mistakes, but love will cover.

Obviously, there are extreme examples of criminal activity where a person's offense and missteps are against the law—a child abuser, sexual predator, drug dealer, etc. For the safety and well-being of others, these types of people need to be exposed to the authorities, but the manner in which they are exposed and the spirit in which this is done is important. Love will expose them for their benefit and the well-being of others.

If you choose to gossip, criticize, murmur and take offense regarding the faults of your friend, what are you promoting?

_____

We all have imperfections and areas in our lives that need growth. Thank God that as we desire to walk in the light of His Word and please Him,

He is patient and kind towards us. He's merciful and forgiving. We need to give that same type of love, mercy and forgiveness to our friends.

2.   Colossians 3:13

Underline the words "forgive" and "forgave."

You must make allowance for each other's faults and forgive the person who offends you. Remember, the Lord forgave you, so you must forgive others. NLT

What are we supposed to remember? _____

What are we supposed to make allowances for? _____

_____

Who are we to forgive? _____

#9.   Miss Outdoor Café: Friends That Share Your Love For God

One of my favorite things to do is to sit in a sunny outdoor café with my dear friends and share God stuff for hours. It's encouraging, educational and exciting to hear what God is doing in the lives of my friends. I love to hear about what God has been speaking to their hearts or what He's shown them in the Word. I love to talk about vision, reaching the lost, fresh revelations from the Word, serving God and influencing others for Christ. We need those kinds of friends in our lives and we need to be that kind of friend; the kind that draws the conversation toward the things of God at appropriate times. Conversations like this are like a God-rush; I love it! Apparently, God likes it too.

The best kind of friend is the kind you can sit on a porch and swing with, never say a word, and then walk away feeling like it was the best conversation you ever had. Unknown

1.   Malachi 3:16

Underline the phrase "lives honored God."

Then those whose lives honored GOD got together and talked it over. GOD saw what they were doing and listened in. A book was opened in God's presence and minutes were taken of the meeting, with the names of the GOD-fearers written down, all the names of those who honored GOD's name. The Message

What did these Christian friends do? _____

_____

Who was listening to their conversation? _____

What did God do? _____

Describe the last "God-talk" you had with one of your friends. _____

_____

_____

⋙Nugget⋙ God recorded it! Isn't that the coolest thought? I am a books person, so the idea that God would listen to a conversation that my friends and I had about Him and then record it, just fires me up! I can just imagine an entire wing of God's massive, heavenly library to be filled with "Conversation Books."

So, let's give Him something to write about! The next time you and your girl friends get together, take the initiative to move the conversation toward the things of God. Ask interesting questions to hear what He is doing in their lives.

2.   2 Timothy 1:16-18

Underline the phrases that describe the way Onesiphorus encouraged Paul in the Lord.

16 The Lord grant mercy to the household of Onesiphorus, for he often refreshed me, and was not ashamed of my chain; 17 but when he arrived in Rome, he sought me out very zealously and found me. 18 The Lord grant to him that he may find mercy from the Lord in that Day — and you know very well how many ways he ministered to me at Ephesus. NKJV

Onesiphorus knew of Paul's suffering in ministry and perhaps he thought Paul might be discouraged, so he took the initiative to find and encourage Paul. He ministered to Paul. As Paul was refreshed he could continue to preach the gospel. Onesiphorus must have kept tabs on Paul's life and ministry—perhaps he was a prayer warrior, a ministry partner or just a dear friend. In any event, he was a blessing to Paul.

Describe the role of "taking the initiative" in friendship. _____

What did Onesiphorus do for Paul? _____

Sometimes, as we share Christ with others we face persecution from our families, friends or co-workers. That's when it's nice to have a friend to root us on in the Lord. It's a blessing to have a friend that loves God and shares the same passion for the gospel.

❧**Nugget**❧ Godly friends can provide official or unofficial accountability for us. We need people that will hold us accountable in our walk with God. If we know someone is going to ask about our spiritual life, we are motivated to stay consistent in our quiet times and prayer life.

3.   Psalm 16:3

Underline the phrase "my true heroes."

The godly people in the land are my true heroes! I take pleasure in them! NLT

Listen to how the Message Bible puts it . . .

"And these God-chosen lives all around — what splendid friends they make!" The Message

What type of friends are our heroes? _____

God certainly wants us to reach out to the lost, unchurched and seekers. Jesus told us to *"Go ye into all the world and preach the gospel to every creature . . ."* and that is what we should do. Cultivating relationships with those who do not know Jesus, with the hope of leading them to Him, is to be an important part of our relational world.

ॐ**Nugget**ॐ Think about your circle of friends. Do you have a strong group of Christian friends you relate to? On one hand, we are all in the family of God and we ought to love and relate easily to everyone in the Body of Christ, regardless of common interests. At the same time, we all seek to find or belong to a small group or circle of friends where we share similar interests. I have found that often in the Christian world and in church, people come and go and never really find "their people." For some reason, it seems that because of insecurities or false ideas we assume that others are not interested in us, or they are more spiritual than we are, or smarter, richer, more together and they certainly wouldn't want to be our friend. That is a lie from the pit and it has robbed people of rich friendships. It's true that all of us relate to different kinds of people. Generally, when a person enters a crowded room, church service, party or social setting, they immediately scan the room to find "their people." In other words, often we look for people in our general age range and a similar season of life and those we have something in common with. In the church world, when people don't find "their people" immediately, they often quit looking and then they fade from fellowship with Christians. Church attendance wanes, small group involvement, serving and the social component of their Christian life dries up. It doesn't take long before one day they look around and wonder why they don't have any strong, on-fire, hip Christian friends.

I encourage you to be proactive in seeking Christian friends. Make it a point to attend events where "your people" would be—church services, small groups, Bible studies, women's events and other environments where God can connect you to other dynamic Christian gals. The Lord wants you and I to have deep, heartfelt friendships with other believers; people who share our love for God. It's needed. It's healthy and we should cultivate and take pleasure in the godly friends God has put in our lives.

#10. Miss Pantyhose: Friends That Stick With You

Pantyhose are a blessing and a drag. My most embarrassing moment revolves around pantyhose. It happened one Sunday. I was single, getting ready for church and decided to wear a new dress I had purchased. I loved that dress. I was running late and in a hurry to get to church. When I flew into the worship service, they were in the middle of the worship set and everyone was still standing and singing. I found my family and slid into the pew area to sing. After praise and worship when the pastor asked everyone to greet one another and have a seat, I realized the most dreadful thing had happened. When I went to smooth out the back of my dress and sit down, something did not feel right! It was then that I realized I had tucked my dress **and** my slip inside my pantyhose! I was mortified! I had just spent the past few minutes singing my praises to God, while my backside was freaking out the

It marks a big step in your development when you come to realize that other people can help you do a better job than you could do alone.
Andrew Carnegie

people behind me. I was so embarrassed; I never heard another thing the preacher said that day!

Pantyhose have a way of sticking. We need friends who will stick with us through thick or thin.

1.   Proverbs 17:17

Underline the phrase "friends love."

Friends love through all kinds of weather, and families stick together in all kinds of trouble. The Message

When do friends love us? _____

Don't be a "fair weather" friend; stick it out through every season. There inevitably are seasons and transitions in friendship, but be the type of friend that doesn't bail when the chips are down.

2.   Proverbs 18:24

Underline the phrase "a true friend."

Friends come and friends go, but a true friend sticks by you like family. The Message

What's the difference between a "friend" and a "true friend"? _____

_____

Make a list of your "friends." _____

_____

Make a list of your "true friends." _____

_____

Scriptures To Chew On

Taking time to meditate on and memorize God's Word is invaluable. Hiding His Word in our hearts will strengthen us for the present and arm us for the future. Here are two verses to memorize and chew on this week. Write these verses on index cards and carry them with you this week. If you will post them in your bathroom, dashboard, desk, locker or other convenient places, you will find these Scriptures taking root in your heart.

> *"Just as lotions and fragrance give sensual delight,*
> *a sweet friendship refreshes the soul."*
> *Proverbs 27:9, The Message*

> *"Then those whose lives honored GOD got together and talked it over.*
> *GOD saw what they were doing and listened in.*
> *A book was opened in God's presence and minutes were taken*
> *of the meeting, with the names of the GOD-fearers written down,*
> *all the names of those who honored GOD's name."*
> *Malachi 3:16, The Message*

Group Discussion

1. In the "Ten Most Wanted" friends, which three traits do you desire most in the friends in your life? Why?

2. In the "Ten Most Wanted" friends, which three traits do you need to improve on the most? Why?

3. Describe the blessing of having a friend(s) that share your love for God. Can you describe a season where you did not have this type of friend? Share the way you found this type of friend.

Maria in Japan

Scott & his sister dealing with
    their Mom

Alhzeimer Disease

Quin Bryan.

Ben - overwhelmed & anxious.

Maybe you are wondering, *"How? How can I be a better friend? How can I start sowing some friend seeds? How can I improve my current friendships?"* If you're feeling like a flabby friend, it's time to hit God's Gym and work the friendship building workout stations circuit. Have you ever been to Curves, the workout place for women? You rotate through a variety of stations giving your body a 20-30 minute workout. Other gyms are similar—you spend a certain amount of time on each machine at each station to get the body you want. Good news! The Bible gives us a great friendship workout, guaranteed to define and build your friendship muscles.

The 12 "One Another" Stations

In order to make this work as a regular part of your life, it is going to require two major, honkin' paradigm changes. Are you ready?

First, it's your attitude. You will have to shift from the *"Here I am"* perspective to the *"There you are"* approach. That means in all of your relational dealings, it's not about you; it's about them. Your focus isn't on how you look, sound or appear, or on what you are going to say, share or do, but rather on the person or people you are with and how you can enrich their lives, by practically incorporating the "One Another" workout into your relational life. Got it?

Listen to this encouragement. *"Is there any such thing as Christians cheering each other up? Do you love me enough to want to help me? Does it mean anything to*

Love
is
a
better
master
than
duty.
Albert
Einstein

you that we are brothers in the Lord, sharing the same Spirit? Are your hearts tender and sympathetic at all? Then make me truly happy by loving each other and agreeing wholeheartedly with each other, working together with one heart and mind and purpose. Don't be selfish; don't live to make a good impression on others. Be humble, thinking of others as better than yourself. Don't just think about your own affairs, but be interested in others, too, and in what they are doing." Philippians 2:1-4, TLB One more . . . *"Let no one seek his own, but each one the other's well-being." 1 Corinthians 10:24, NKJV*

Second, you've got to get dressed! Here's the Designer outfit. *"So, chosen by God for this new life of love, dress in the wardrobe God picked out for you: compassion, kindness, humility, quiet strength, discipline. Be even-tempered, content with second place, quick to forgive an offense. Forgive as quickly and completely as the Master forgave you. And regardless of what else you put on, wear love. It's your basic, all-purpose garment. Never be without it." Colossians 3:12-14, The Message*

Okay, now that our attitudes are changed and we're dressed, let's hit God's gym and work it out.

Station #1: Love One Another

This is the most important station. Let's look at several verses of Scripture in the New Testament to see how many times this is reiterated.

1.   John 13:34, 15:12, 15:17

        Underline the phrase "love one another."

        13:34 A new commandment I give unto you, that ye love one another; as I have loved you, that ye also love one another . . . 15:12 This is my commandment, That ye love one another, as I have loved you . . . 15:17 These things I command you, that ye love one another. KJV

It is easy to love those that are lovable.

What is Jesus' new commandment for New Testament believers? _____

That we love one another

How are we to love one another? *As He loves us.*

_____

The good news under the New Testament is that we only have to keep one command, rather than thousands of commandments. The one command is to love!

2. Romans 13:8

Underline the phrase "love one another."

Owe no man any thing, but to <u>love one another:</u> for he that loveth another hath fulfilled the law. KJV

If we want to fulfill all of God's requirements under the Old Testament Law, what must we do?

Love one another.

3. 1 Thessalonians 4:9

Underline the phrase "love one another."

But as touching brotherly love ye need not that I write unto you: for ye yourselves are taught of God to <u>love one another.</u> KJV

Who teaches us to love one another? *God*

What are some practical ways to love others? *Be respectful, show kindness, not judgemental, have time for our friends - time with them is having a heart for them.*

4.   1 John 3:11, 23 and 4:7-12

Underline the phrase "love one another."

11 For this is the message that ye heard from the beginning, that we should <u>love one another</u> . . . 23 And this is his commandment, That we should believe on the name of his Son Jesus Christ, and <u>love one another</u>, as he gave us commandment . . . 7 Beloved, let us <u>love one another</u>: for love is of God; and every one that loveth is born of God, and knoweth God. 8 He that loveth not knoweth not God; for God is love. 9 In this was manifested the love of God toward us, because that God sent his only begotten Son into the world, that we might live through him. 10 Herein is love, not that we loved God, but that he loved us, and sent his Son to be the propitiation for our sins. 11 Beloved, if God so loved us, we ought also to <u>love one another.</u> 12 No man hath seen God at any time. If we <u>love one another</u>, God dwelleth in us, and his love is perfected in us. KJV

Where does love originate? <u>*In God*</u>

Who loved first? <u>*God*</u>

If God loved us, how does that enable us to love others? <u>*By example*</u>

In practical terms, how can we love one another? <u>*Be respectful, Show kindness, help one another. Take the time to take care for one another.*</u>

5.   1 Peter 1:22

Underline the phrase "love one another."

Seeing ye have purified your souls in obeying the truth through the Spirit unto unfeigned love of the brethren, see that ye <u>love one another</u> with a pure heart fervently . . . KJV

According to this passage, how are we to love one another? _____

_____

6.   2 John 5

Underline the phrase "love one another."

And now I beseech thee, lady, not as though I wrote a new commandment unto thee, but that which we had from the beginning, that we <u>love one another</u>. KJV

One more time, what is the new commandment?

To love one another

A friend loves at all times. Proverbs 17:17

Get the idea? Over and over Jesus and the writers of the New Testament emphasized the importance of loving God and loving one another as Jesus loves us. This is the command we are to obey as New Testament believers. You don't have to remember the Ten Commandments and you don't have to remember the hundreds of Old Testament laws; you only have to remember the New Commandment which is summed up as loving God and loving others. It's easy to remember, but will take your entire spirit, soul and body to obey!

Station #2: Be Devoted To One Another

1.   Romans 12:10

Underline the phrase "be devoted to one another."

Be devoted to one another in brotherly love . . . NIV

How would you define "devoted"? _Dedicated_

2.   1 Corinthians 16:15

Underline the phrase "devoted themselves."

I urge you, brethren — you know the household of Stephanas, that it is the firstfruits of Achaia, and that they have devoted themselves to the ministry of the saints . . . NKJV

What did this family devote themselves to? _the ministry of the Saints_

Station #3: Accept One Another

1.   Romans 15:7

Underline the phrase "accept one another."

Accept one another, then, just as Christ accepted you, in order to bring praise to God. NIV

How should we accept one another? _as Christ did_

Describe this in real life. _Remember that we are all God's children and that He sees good in all of us._

2.	Romans 14:13

Underline the phrase "judge one another."

Let us not therefore judge one another any more . . . KJV

What are we not to do to one another? _____

☙**Nugget**❧: When we choose to accept one another, flaws and all, we are walking in God's love. To accept one another does not necessarily mean that we condone all behavior. There are certain personalities that rub us the wrong way. People have idiosyncrasies that can seem odd. There may be some people that you don't "like" per se, but we are commanded to love and accept one another.

Describe a scenario where you've had to accept someone that rubbed you the wrong way or that you didn't particularly "like."

_____

_____

Station #4: Instruct One Another

1.	Romans 15:14

Underline the phrase "instruct one another."

I myself am convinced, my brothers, that you yourselves are full of goodness, complete in knowledge and competent to instruct one another. NIV

What makes a person competent to instruct others, according to this verse?

_____

2. Colossians 3:16

Underline the phrase "instruct and direct one another."

Let the Word of Christ — the Message — have the run of the house. Give it plenty of room in your lives. Instruct and direct one another using good common sense. And sing, sing your hearts out to God! The Message

What gives us the ability to instruct and direct one another, according to this verse?

_____

๙**Nugget**๛ If we are humble and teachable, we can learn from just about anyone. I love learning from others and hearing the things the Lord has shared with them. Anytime someone sheds new light on the Scriptures or shares a nugget of truth from the Word, I am blessed. The only caveat in instructing one another is to be sure that we don't start to "preach at" our friends; that gets annoying! Talking to and sharing with our friends is great, but very few people appreciate being preached at if it is not solicited.

Station #5: Serve One Another

1. Galatians 5:13-14

Underline the phrase "serve one another."

13 You, my brothers, were called to be free. But do not use your freedom to indulge the sinful nature; rather, serve one another in love. 14 The entire law is summed up in a single command: "Love your neighbor as yourself." NIV

Who in your life could you do a better job serving? _____

_____

In what ways can we serve one another? _____

_____

&**Nugget**& Serving others is love in action. Acts of service is the love language of some people, according to Gary Chapman in his book *The Five Love Languages.*[1] Making meals, cleaning the home, washing the car, doing the laundry, serving a cup of coffee, carrying the luggage, making breakfast in bed and other gestures of service come easily and naturally for those who find acts of service as their primary love language. The rest of us really have to be on the lookout for the needs around us and ways to serve others.

2.   1 Peter 4:10

Underline the phrase "serve others."

Each one should use whatever gift he has received to serve others, faithfully administering God's grace in its various forms. NIV

What gifts and talents has God graced you with and how are you using these things to serve others?

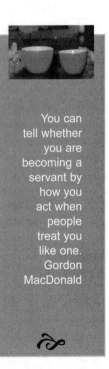

You can tell whether you are becoming a servant by how you act when people treat you like one. Gordon MacDonald

_____

_____

_____

_____

Station #6: Bear With One Another

1.   Ephesians 4:1-2

Underline the phrase "bearing with one another."

Be completely humble and gentle; be patient, bearing with one another in love. NIV

What do you think it means to "bear" with others? _____

_____

Forbearing: The word "bearing" in the King James Bible is the word "forbearing," and according to Strong's Concordance this means "to hold oneself up against." Figuratively, it means to put up with. It's also translated to mean "bear with," "endure" and "suffer."[2]

Have you had to bear with someone while they went through a difficult time, grief, transition or dramatic life change? Have you ever had to put up with someone at a family reunion, office party, neighborhood barbecue? Ever had to bear with someone during their time of weakness, repentance and the recovery process? Had to endure a certain person's personality or quirks? Patiently supported and suffered through things with an individual? If so, you were "bearing with one another in love"!

2.   Colossians 3:13

Underline the phrase "bear with each other."

Bear with each other and forgive whatever grievances you may have against one another. Forgive as the Lord forgave you. NIV

What other act of love seems to accompany bearing with one another?

_____

Often as we put up with people, we find that we have to extend a lot of forgiveness and grace.

Do you have people in your life that you just have to endure and put up with? If so, how will you be better at bearing with them?

_____

_____

Station #7: Be Affectionate With One Another

1.   1 Peter 5:14

Underline the phrase "salute one another with a kiss."

Salute one another with a kiss of love [the symbol of mutual affection].
AMP

How would you describe this display of affection? _____

Are there times when "a kiss of love" would not be appropriate? When?

_____

_____

In what ways can you extend Christ-like affection to those around you in appropriate ways, without being uncomfortably "touchy" or "ice cold"?

_____

_____

In some cultures kissing others is quite common. Men kiss men on both sides of the cheek as do the women. In other cultures, friends will greet one another with a handshake, hug or embrace. In the church world, we've seen some people who are "huggy and kissy" to everyone they meet, and for some folks this is quite uncomfortable. We've also seen other folks that were so stiff and stoic you didn't know if they loved you or hated you. God wants us to greet one another with brotherly love in an authentic and affectionate way.

2.   1 Thessalonians 2:8

Underline the phrase "an affection for you."

Having so fond an affection for you, we were well-pleased to impart to you not only the gospel of God but also our own lives, because you had become very dear to us. NASU

Having affection for others will lead us to impart what two things?

_____

_____

Station #8: Be Kind To One Another

1.   Ephesians 4:32

Underline the phrase "kind one to another."

And be ye kind one to another, tenderhearted . . . KJV

How would you define "kind" and "tenderhearted"? _____

_____

2.   1 Corinthians 13:4

Underline the phrase "love is kind."

Love is patient, love is kind. It does not envy, it does not boast, it is not proud. NIV

Love is what? _____

Love does not do what? _____

Station #9: Be Forgiving To One Another

1. Ephesians 4:32

    Underline the phrase "forgiving one another."

    . . . forgiving one another, even as God for Christ's sake hath forgiven you. KJV

    Have you ever needed forgiveness? _____

    Has God forgiven you? _____

    How are we to forgive one another?

    _____

    _____

    Can you hold a grudge or unforgiveness against anyone, when Jesus has forgiven you of all your sins?

    _____

    Jesus told us to forgive anyone of anything! If we ever think we have the right to withhold forgiveness from anyone for anything, we need to reread Mark 11:25-26, pronto!

Three things in life are important. The first is to be kind. The second is to be kind. The third is to be kind.
Henry James

2.	Colossians 3:13

Underline the words "forgive whatever" and "against one another."

. . . forgive whatever grievances you may have against one another. Forgive as the Lord forgave you. NIV

According to this verse, what grievances are you allowed to maintain?

_____

Station #10: Comfort One Another

1.	1 Thessalonians 4:18

Underline the phrase "comfort one another."

Wherefore <u>comfort one another</u> with these words. KJV

What can we comfort others with? *Our words & actions ability to listen*

In this passage, the Apostle Paul was specifically telling the readers that they could comfort one another with words about Jesus' second coming and our eternal destiny with Jesus. Other passages in the Bible and particularly in Proverbs tell us that our words can literally comfort and minister grace and pleasantness to the hearer. Use your mouth to comfort others!

2.	1 Thessalonians 5:11

Underline the phrase "comfort yourselves" and "edify one another."

Wherefore comfort yourselves together, and edify one another, even as also ye do. KJV

How can we comfort and edify one another? _____

Again, one way we can give comfort and edification is through our words. Read Ephesians 4:29 for a great description of the power of our words.

Station #11: Exhort One Another

1.   Hebrews 3:13

Underline the phrase "exhort one another."

But exhort one another daily, while it is called Today; lest any of you be hardened through the deceitfulness of sin. KJV

How often should we exhort others? _____

Why is it necessary to be exhorted? _____

_____

How would you define "exhort"? _____

_____

Exhort: From the Greek word "parakaleoo," its meaning includes to admonish, to beg, entreat, beseech, console, encourage, comfort and strengthen by consolation.[3]

2.   Hebrews 10:24-25

Underline the phrases "consider one another" and "exhorting one another."

Remove oneself from the situation

24 And let us consider one another to provoke unto love and to good works: 25 Not forsaking the assembling of ourselves together, as the manner of some is; but exhorting one another: and so much the more, as ye see the day approaching. KJV

What are we to provoke one another to do? _____

What are we to encourage people not to forsake? _____

Describe the intensity and frequency with which we should be exhorting one another.

_____

Nugget One of the enemy's most effective snares is to convince, distract and turn people from going to church where they will gather with other believers for worship, the Word and strength for their God-given assignment. Often the greatest trap people fall into is busyness and apathy. They get busy with their jobs, sports and leisure and justify their inconsistent and non-existent church attendance with rationalizations like, *"Sunday is our only day off and we want to spend it with (pick one) our kids, doing yard work, sleeping, watching TV and football games, reading, counting the carpet fibers in our family room, watching the grass grow . . ."* you name it! Or you will hear people make apathetic comments like, *"I don't need church, God can talk to me and my family at home just fine. I connect with God better when I am (pick one) enjoying God's creation, fishing, skiing, boating, cleaning, painting, sleeping, digging a hole to China. . ."* you name it! If it wasn't so sad, it would be humorous.

As one preacher said, the reality is that when you have a bonfire all the logs glow brightly and stay ablaze. But when you pull one log off the fire and set it aside, it's just a matter of time until the log loses its fire. It's the same with our faith. When we are regularly attending church, worshipping God, growing in the Word and reaching out to others, we stay aglow with God's Spirit. But when we quit attending church our flame begins to go out and grow cold like the lone log.

We need to be exhorted and we need to exhort others to get into church on a regular basis. If you are drying up on the vine, spiritually speaking, stir yourself up and find an on-fire, Word- and worship-driven church with a heart to reach a city, and get busy doing something for God!

Station #12: Honor One Another

1. Romans 12:10

    Underline the phrase "honor one another."

    . . . Honor one another above yourselves. NIV

    How should we honor others? _Valuing them_

    In your own words, how do you define "honor"? _By showing them with words and actions that they are important to me. Being extra kind and gentle._

Honor: The Greek word for honor is *time,* and its meaning includes a value, esteem, precious. [4]

In what ways can you honor others?

Showing them with words and actions that they are precious

&**Nugget**& We live in a casual society, and in some ways that has been a good thing. But in other ways our casual attitude has translated into disrespect and dishonor towards others. When we were kids, we were taught to address adults by Mr. and Mrs., we were taught to respect authority and to honor the office a person held. Today, kids call adults by their first names, authority is

You can make more friends in two months by becoming really interested in other people, than you can in two years by trying to get other people interested in you.
Bernard Meltzer

dismissed and people don't know the spiritual implications of honoring the office of the President, the police, the boss, the teacher, ministry offices including apostle, prophet, evangelist, pastor and teacher. When we esteem others as valuable and precious and validate that with our actions, we are showing honor.

2.   Galatians 5:26

Underline these words: "vainglorious," "self-conceited," "competitive," "challenging," "provoking," "irritating," "envying" and "jealous."

Let us not become vainglorious and self-conceited, competitive and challenging and provoking and irritating to one another, envying and being jealous of one another. AMP

What should we avoid? _____

In your friendships, where do you need to improve? *In the areas of competitiveness and envy.*

Scriptures To Chew On

Taking time to meditate on and memorize God's Word is invaluable. Hiding His Word in our hearts will strengthen us for the present and arm us for the future. Here are two verses to memorize and chew on this week. Write these verses on index cards and carry them with you this week. If you will post them in your bathroom, dashboard, desk, locker or other convenient places, you will find these Scriptures taking root in your heart.

"Let no one seek his own, but each one the other's well-being."
1 Corinthians 10:24, NKJV

"Beloved, let us love one another:
for love is of God;
and every one that loveth is born of God, and knoweth God.
He that loveth not knoweth not God; for God is love."
1 John 4:7-8, KJV

Group Discussion

1. Describe the way you can become a "There you are" type of friend more
    than a "Here I am" friend. *Take a more pro-active*
    approach. Make the call don't wait for it
    to come

2. Which of the 12 One Another Stations do you need to spend more time
    working out at? *Accept One Another*

3. Which one of the 12 One Another Stations is the biggest challenge for
    you? *Be Forgiving to One Another*

[1] Chapman, Gary D. The Five Love Languages. Chicago: Moody Publishers, 1996. (pg 59)

[2] Biblesoft's New Exhaustive Strong's Numbers and Concordance with Expanded Greek-Hebrew Dictionary. Copyright © 1994, 2003 Biblesoft, Inc. and International Bible Translators, Inc.

[3] From Thayer's Greek Lexicon, Electronic Database. Copyright © 2000, 2003 by Biblesoft, Inc. All rights reserved

[4] Biblesoft's, see Footnote 2 above.

Personal Notes

9/27/06

Chris' dad

Jeanie - healing prayers
   her dad - URI

Manny - kidney stone surgery

Quin - surgery

Grace - Ronda's daughter

Connie's Mom's arm broken
      & having a brow lift

Chris (Connie's friend) lost job

Denise - surgery on face

Ann - double masectomy

Chris' - friend cancer genes
            hysterectomy

Katie - dad

H eart friends. Kindred spirit. God-knit. God-breathed friendships. Been praying for a friend? Looking for a bosom buddy? A best friend?

Healthy Friendships

Remember Anne of Green Gables? She wondered:

". . . do you think that I shall ever have a bosom friend . . . ?"

"A—a what kind of friend?"

"A bosom friend—an intimate friend, you know—a really kindred spirit to whom I can confide my inmost soul. I've dreamed of meeting her all my life. I never really supposed I would, but so many of my loveliest dreams have come true all at once that perhaps this one will, too. Do you think it's possible?"[1]

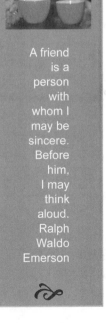

It's possible! Jesus had this type of relationship. Jonathan and David enjoyed this type of friendship. I believe these are special, God-ordained types of friendships. God-knit. God-breathed. If you are married, it's likely that your husband is your best friend and "soul mate," and perhaps you also have a nice circle of gal friends to hang out with. Yet at the same time, I know many women that long for a close chick friend and confidant. I've been blessed to have had three girl friendships, "bosom friends" or Jonathan-David type friendships in my forty-plus years, and in each case God knit our hearts together in such a way that we were almost closer than blood sisters. These types of relationships aren't found everyday. They are not a dime a

A friend is a person with whom I may be sincere. Before him, I may think aloud. Ralph Waldo Emerson

dozen. They are priceless. Treasures. You are blessed if you have one of these types of friendships in your lifetime.

As we've said previously, Jesus enjoyed relationships on all levels: with the multitudes, the twelve, the three (Peter, James and John) and the one (John). We see Jesus minister to the *multitudes* in healing, feeding, preaching and teaching. Then we see Him pour into His *twelve* disciples; He took the *three*, Peter, James and John, with Him to the mount of transfiguration; and then we watch the *one* apostle, John, lay his head on Jesus' chest at the Last Supper.

❧**Nugget**❧   In each of the Jonathan-David friendships I've enjoyed in my life, I have found a few common threads.

First, God had already put Michelle, Mary Jo and Mary in my life before I knew I needed their friendship. Michelle was a high school classmate, Mary Jo was a neighbor and Mary was three of my children's second grade teacher. How nice of the Lord to position these God-friends in our lives! Perhaps it would be a good idea to look at your own life and ask the Lord if he has already put a potential bosom buddy friend in your pathway.

Second, these friends were deeply committed to the Lord and their love for God overflowed into every area of their lives.

Third, I've found that God always has a greater purpose in these type of friendships. A friend of mine has said it this way: *"God always leads us to people who will lead us to Him."* I've observed that the Lord has used each of the Jonathan-David friendships that I have had to bring me to a new place with Him. I believe friendships of this type are mutually beneficial and God uses them to help propel us further in our walk with Him, our prayer life, and in His plan, purpose and destiny for our lives. He gives us these friends to walk through various seasons of life—college, work, marriage, child-rearing, menopause, the ebb and flow of life. It's nice to have a heart friend to call when you need a favor or help with your kids; when you need prayer or a shoulder to cry on; when you need a spiritual kick in the pants or someone to drink a cappie with; or when you need someone to help you paint your kitchen or pray for your husband's new job. Whatever comes, it's a blessing to have a God-breathed friendship! Have you considered His purposes in your friendships? What season of life are you in and how does He want your friendship to add value to your life and theirs? Does He want to lead you into a new place of prayer? Increase your hunger for the Word? Prepare you for ministry or give you a heart for the lost? God uses this type of friendship to lead us to a more mature place in Him.

Fourth, I've always seen these Jonathan-David friendships to be spiritually beneficial and mutually rewarding to all parties. He uses these God-breathed relationships to bless us and make us a blessing—it's a win-win for everyone. Definitely a God-thing!

Do you desire a God-friend like this? I've talked with lots of women over the years and the universal cry I hear is the longing gals have for a "best friend." They love their husbands dearly, but they desire the friendship that other women add to their lives. A chick friend. A prayer partner. A confidant. Most people have acquaintances and co-workers they can chum with, but few woman have one or two unique, heart friends they can confide in.

I believe God wants to answer your desire for a friend, and as you study this lesson, I pray that you receive His wisdom on discovering and cultivating a Jonathan-David friendship. Let's look at the dynamics of a God-breathed friendship, like the one that Jonathan and David enjoyed to see what insights we can glean.

Divine Clickage

1.	1 Samuel 18:1-4

	Underline the phrases "Jonathan became one in spirit with David," and "he loved him as himself."

	1 After David had finished talking with Saul, Jonathan became one in spirit with David, and he loved him as himself. 2 From that day Saul kept David with him and did not let him return to his father's house. 3 And Jonathan made a covenant with David because he loved him as himself. 4 Jonathan took off the robe he was wearing and gave it to

David, along with his tunic, and even his sword, his bow and his belt.
NIV

In verse 1, what caused Jonathan to become one in spirit with David?

_____

In verses 1 and 3, how does this passage describe the love that Jonathan had in his heart for David?

Jonathan became one in spirit o David
He loved him as himself

At this encounter while David was chatting with Jonathan's dad, God put something in Jonathan's heart which initiated what I call "friendship clickage." It seems that God put His love in Jonathan's heart for David. Perhaps, when Jonathan heard David speaking, he liked his personality, heart for God or sense of humor, and God put a love for David inside Jonathan's heart. Sometimes we say it this way when there is clickage: God connects you supernaturally and it's as if you've found "your people"! It's a God-thing.

☙**Nugget**❧ As we've mentioned: *"God always leads us to people who will lead us to Him."* In light of God's call on David to be King of Israel and in light of the difficulties that David was about to face, is it possible that God knit Jonathan's soul to David to be a source of rich and much needed encouragement, wisdom and help? At the same time, we'll see that God knew Jonathan's future as well, and because of the covenant of their friendship, David's love for Jonathan precipitated his care for Jonathan's family. It seems that these Jonathan-David type friendships often have a divine purpose in mutually propelling us into God's will. God knows our future and His calling and purpose, and He brings friends into our lives that help encourage, refresh, protect and motivate us to fulfill our destiny.

Think about it. Are you praying for a God-breathed friend? It's very possible that God has already put this friend in your life and that they are also praying for a Jonathan-David type friend. God's Word says that He knows what we need before we ask Him. He orders our steps and provides everything we need for fulfilling His will in our lives, including rich friendships. When Mary and I became friends a number of years ago, we had both unknowingly been praying for a chick friend for over a year. In God's time and His bigger picture, He put our paths together and knit a great friendship.

Has God put anyone in your life that you find you gravitate towards or just seem to click with? Do you sense God's unconditional love in your heart for someone in your life? Often, if we can locate God's love on the inside of us and then follow His love, it will lead us to people He wants to connect us with.

I have found that in each of the God-breathed friendships the Lord has given me, He put a divine "click" in my heart as I got to know Michelle, Mary Jo and Mary. From my experience and as I've read the Bible, I don't believe that you can manufacture these types of friendships. It's a God-thing.

ఌ**Nugget**ఌ One little caveat . . . relationships and particularly "Jonathan-David Friendships" require a mutual, God-given desire for friendship. For example, at times God will drop His love in your heart for a particular person, not because He wants you to become their friend, but simply because He wants you to pray for them or encourage them. He gives you a snippet of His love, and as you follow His love it will lead you to pray for, lift and encourage those God puts in your heart. On the other hand, at times God will put His love for someone in your heart and at the same time, He will put His love for you in their heart. There is a mutual sense of "divine clickage," and both parties will have a desire to develop a friendship. If God has put someone in

I value the friend who for me finds time on his calendar, but I cherish the friend who for me does not consult his calendar.
Robert Brault

ఌ

your heart but you are not in their heart, don't force it, don't be upset, don't be discouraged. God is the one that gives people a place in our hearts and God is the one that will give you a place in others' hearts. If you want to enjoy His divine plan for friendship, the most important thing you can do is identify who God has put in your heart and then follow His love to be a blessing to them. If He has put you in their heart, they will likely automatically reciprocate and a friendship will begin to blossom.

For example, there have been several occasions where the Lord has put His love for someone in my heart and I felt great compassion for them. I have learned to identify that this love was in my heart simply so I could pray for that person in a particular season of their life, but a friendship with them was not in God's plan. His love in my heart was there purely to motivate me to pray for them. As my husband and I lead our church, God has put me in the hearts of several of our ladies who have been such a blessing to my life and have faithfully prayed for me and lifted me to Lord when I desperately needed it! It was not His plan for us to become bosom buddies, per se, although I love them dearly. He put me in their hearts and that has motivated them to pray for me. I am so thankful! Does this make sense?

Have you experienced this type of friendship where there was a mutual divine click and a God-breathed friendship developed? If so, describe it.

With Lemys.

Have you experienced God's love in your heart for someone for the purpose of motivating you to pray for them?

2. 1 Samuel 19:1-3, 6-7

Underline the phrase "Jonathan was very fond of David."

1 Saul told his son Jonathan and all the attendants to kill David. But Jonathan was very fond of David 2 and warned him, "My father Saul is looking for a chance to kill you. Be on your guard tomorrow morning; go into hiding and stay there. 3 I will go out and stand with my father in the field where you are. I'll speak to him about you and will tell you what I find out." . . . 6 Saul listened to Jonathan and took this oath: "As surely as the LORD lives, David will not be put to death." 7 So Jonathan called David and told him the whole conversation. He brought him to Saul, and David was with Saul as before. NIV

I love how the New King James Version brings out 1 Samuel 19:1.

Now Saul spoke to Jonathan his son and to all his servants, that they should kill David; but Jonathan, Saul's son, delighted greatly in David. NKJV

How does verse 1 describe Jonathan's heart toward David? _____

Jonathan's heart delighted greatly in David

❧**Nugget**❧ Notice that God-ordained friendships are "delightful." We've all experienced relationships that are draining, high maintenance and a lot of work. It's wonderful to find friends that refresh and delight your heart and bring you joy. All relationships take work, but there are certain friendships that tend to be more draining than refreshing. When God knits your heart together in a "Jonathan-David" type of friendship, there is a sense of delight that tends to energize and refresh you, rather than drain and sap you. You look forward to getting together, rather than dreading it!

In verse 1, Jonathan's father Saul had become very jealous of David's success and wanted to kill him, and it's obvious that Jonathan's friendship with David superseded the relationship Jonathan had with his own father.

Because of his love, what did Jonathan do for David? _____

_____

Jonathan was fond of David and he worked hard to protect David from his own father's evil agenda.

Divine Commitment

1.   1 Samuel 20:1-42

Underline the phrases "I have found favor in your eyes," "Whatever you want me to do, I'll do for you," "he loved him as he loved himself" and "we have sworn friendship with each other in the name of the LORD."

1 Then David fled from Naioth at Ramah and went to Jonathan and asked, "What have I done? What is my crime? How have I wronged your father, that he is trying to take my life?" 2 "Never!" Jonathan replied. "You are not going to die! Look, my father doesn't do anything, great or small, without confiding in me. Why would he hide this from me? It's not so!" 3 But David took an oath and said, "Your father knows very well that I have found favor in your eyes, and he has said to himself, 'Jonathan must not know this or he will be grieved.' Yet as surely as the LORD lives and as you live, there is only a step between me and death." 4 Jonathan said to David, "Whatever you want me to do, I'll do for you." . . . 12 Then Jonathan said to David: "By the LORD, the God of Israel, I will surely sound out my father by this time the day after tomorrow! If he is favorably disposed toward you, will I not send you word and let you know? . . . 16 So Jonathan made a covenant with the house of David, saying, "May the LORD call David's enemies to account." 17 And Jonathan had David reaffirm his oath out of love for him, because he loved him as he loved himself . . . 23 And about the matter you and I discussed-remember, the LORD is witness between you and me forever." . . . 27 But the next day, the second day of the month, David's place was empty again. Then Saul said to his son Jonathan, "Why hasn't the son of Jesse come to the meal, either yesterday or today?" 28 Jonathan answered, "David earnestly asked me for permission to go to Bethlehem. 29 He said, 'Let me go, because our family is observing a sacrifice in the town and my brother has ordered me to be there. If I have found favor in your eyes, let me get away to see my brothers.' That is why he has not come to the king's table." 30 Saul's anger flared up at Jonathan and he said to him, "You son of a perverse and rebellious woman! Don't I know that you have sided with the son of Jesse to your own shame and to the shame of the mother who bore you? 31 As long as the son of Jesse lives on this earth, neither you nor your kingdom will be established. Now send and bring him to me, for he must die!" 32 "Why should he be put to death? What has he done?" Jonathan asked his father. 33 But Saul hurled his spear at him to kill him. Then Jonathan knew that his father intended to kill David . . . 35 In the morning Jonathan went out to the field for his meeting with David. He had a small boy with him . . . 40 Then Jonathan gave his weapons to the boy and said, "Go, carry them back to town." 41 After the boy had gone, David got up from the south side [of the stone] and bowed down before Jonathan three times, with his face to the ground. Then they kissed each other and wept together-but David wept the most. 42 Jonathan said to David, "Go in peace, for we have sworn friendship with each other in the name of the LORD, saying, 'The LORD is witness between you and me, and between your descendants and my descendants forever.'" Then David left, and Jonathan went back to the town. NIV

One loyal friend is worth ten thousand relatives. Euripides (408 B.C.)

Why did Saul want to kill David? (vs 1, 30-33) _____

_____

_____

In verses 2, 4, 12, 16-17, 23, 28-29, 32-33, 35, 40-42 what was Jonathan's commitment to David?

_____

_____

In verse 4, 16-17, 41-42, we get a picture of the heartfelt love that Jonathan and David had for one another.

Describe how Jonathan felt about David. _____

_____

Describe how David felt about Jonathan. _____

_____

Notice how vulnerable they were and how freely they communicated their affection and commitment to love and bless one another and their families.

☙**Nugget**❧ One secret to lasting, heartfelt, rich relationships is a commitment to communicate. This includes being vulnerable, being interested, being honest and being transparent. It's impossible to have a strong relationship with anyone without a deep level of communication that goes beyond the casual, surface chit-chat. To communicate requires risk. In my closest friendships we have always verbalized our willingness to commit to honest communication! Are you willing to commit yourself to rich communication in your closest relationships?

2.   1 Samuel 23:15-18

Underline the phrase "The two of them made a covenant before the LORD."

15 While David was at Horesh in the Desert of Ziph, he learned that Saul had come out to take his life. 16 And Saul's son Jonathan went to David at Horesh and helped him find strength in God. 17 "Don't be afraid," he said. "My father Saul will not lay a hand on you. You will be king over Israel, and I will be second to you. Even my father Saul knows this." 18 The two of them made a covenant before the LORD. Then Jonathan went home, but David remained at Horesh. NIV

In what way did Jonathan continue to encourage David? _____

_____

What type of covenant did Jonathan and David make? _____

_____

They had agreed that the Lord would watch between them and help them to protect and care for each other's families.

Jonathan was actually the legal heir to the throne, but because he recognized God's anointing on David, how did he prefer and honor David?

_____

❧**Nugget**❧ If we are not on guard, sometimes jealousy, ego and competition or possessiveness can sneak in on our friendships. Jonathan was the legal heir to the throne, but because he recognized God's hand and anointing on David and because he loved David, he was willing to humble himself and prefer David over himself. That takes maturity and God's love. Jonathan didn't want his own will for his life nor for David's; he wanted what God wanted.

Have you recognized God's hand, grace and anointing on your friends? If you find that they are called to something other than you, or more influential or more honored than you (as was the case with Jonathan and David), are you willing to put your own ego and desire down to encourage your friend in God's will?

3.   2 Samuel 1:11-12, 25-27

Underline the phrase "Your love for me was wonderful, more wonderful than that of women."

11 Then David and all the men with him took hold of their clothes and tore them. 12 They mourned and wept and fasted till evening for Saul and his son Jonathan, and for the army of the LORD and the house of Israel, because they had fallen by the sword . . .25 "How the mighty have fallen in battle! Jonathan lies slain on your heights. 26 I grieve for you, Jonathan my brother; you were very dear to me. Your love for me was wonderful, more wonderful than that of women. 27 "How the mighty have fallen! The weapons of war have perished!" NIV

After Jonathan death's, David mourned deeply.

What did David say about his friendship with Jonathan? _____

_____

God wants to knit friendships together in Him. He wants us to enjoy the blessings that come from transparent and committed friendships, within healthy boundaries.

I encourage you to pray and believe God for divine Jonathan-David friendships in your life. I have found that these types of friendships are rare. I thank God for blessing me with my own Jonathan-David type of friendships, as well as dozens of very rich and meaningful friendships on a variety of other levels.

☙**Nugget**☙ Let's take a moment to talk about gay issues: homosexuality and lesbianism. Sometimes, people try to make the relationship that Jonathan and David had into something that it wasn't. They were not gay. They were unashamed of their deep love for one another, the covenant they had made between them and their families, and the affection they shared. Unfortunately, if two men these days talked and behaved the way Jonathan and David did in friendship, people might assume they were gay. Sometimes homophobia keeps men from enjoying God-knit friendships for fear it would seem odd to others. Women are generally more verbal and demonstrative about their affections, so it is not unusual for girls to have deeper friendships than men.

According to Dee Brestin's book, *The Friendships Of Women,* there are a few warning signs that you should consider in this area of homosexuality.[2] If you find yourself having a strong desire for inappropriate or unnatural physical contact with members of the same sex, this is a warning light you should pay attention to. Embraces and natural gestures of affection are healthy, but if it crosses the line and you recognize your desires to be unnatural, it's time to wake up and recognize the snare of the enemy and your own flesh, urging you to move away from what is natural in exchange for what is unnatural.

If you find that your thoughts are consumed with thinking about the other person in an obsessive, unnatural and unhealthy way, pay attention to this warning sign as well. The enemy would love for you to worship the people you love, and twist the love you feel for someone into idolatry and "worshipping created things."

Remember what Romans 1 says about people choosing to invent their own ideas about God and live in a way that is contrary to His Word: *"Because of this, God gave them over to shameful lusts. Even their women exchanged natural relations for unnatural ones. In the same way the men also abandoned natural relations with women and were inflamed with lust for one another. Men committed indecent acts with other men, and received in themselves the due penalty for their perversion." Romans 1:26-27 NIV*

Every man passes his life in the search after friendship. Ralph Waldo Emerson

If you are struggling in the area of homosexuality and desire God's help and freedom, you may want to visit *www.exodus-international.org,* a ministry focused on helping those who want freedom from homosexuality and lesbianism.

Scriptures To Chew On

Taking time to meditate on and memorize God's Word is invaluable. Hiding His Word in our hearts will strengthen us for the present and arm us for the future. Here are two verses to memorize and chew on this week. Write these verses on index cards and carry them with you this week. If you will post them in your bathroom, dashboard, desk, locker or other convenient places, you will find these Scriptures taking root in your heart.

> " . . . *for we have sworn friendship with each other in the name of the LORD, saying, 'The LORD is witness between you and me . . .'"*
> *1 Samuel 20:42, NIV*

> *"I have called you friends, for everything that I learned from my Father I have made known to you."*
> *John 15:15, NIV*

Group Discussion

1.   Describe any Jonathan-David type friendships the Lord has given you and the divine clickage that started your friendship.

2.   Describe the level of commitment and communication in your Jonathan-David friendships. In what ways is it different than other friendships?

3.   In addition to the joy and delight of a God-breathed friendship, have you recognized God's divine purpose in your friendship?

---

[1]Anne of Green Gables.

[2]Brestin, Dee. The Friendships Of Women. Colorado Springs, CO: Chariot Victor Publishing, 1997.

Who's On Your Boat?

God-knit, God-connected friends are truly one of God's best gifts while we live on Planet Earth. Unfortunately, on the other side of the coin there are also dysfunctional and detrimental friendships. Are you troubled by unhealthy relationships? What toxic friendships are you enduring? What manipulative or co-dependant relationships are you trapped in? Yes, while God wants us to enjoy rich friendships, there are times when a relationship has run its course or taken an unhealthy turn, and we need to set boundaries or perhaps walk away.

Because believers feel obligated to turn the other cheek, walk in love, tolerate, go the extra mile, and love their enemies, they often put up with manipulative, toxic, unhealthy, abusive, co-dependent, draining, destructive, controlling and unhealthy relationships in the name of God's love. They put demands on themselves in relationships that even God Himself does not expect. Certainly, there are times when we do need to walk in love, forgive, turn the other cheek, bless our enemies and be all things to all men in order to win them to Christ; there are also times when we need to recognize the nature of a relationship and operate in truth and tough love. In their excellent book, *Boundaries*, Drs. Henry Cloud and John Townsend teach us how to set healthy boundaries with our parents, spouse, friends, co-workers and even ourselves![1]

What does the Bible say about the type of friends you need to steer clear of? The book of Jonah sheds an interesting light on taking inventory of those traveling on your boat.

The best way to destroy an enemy is to make him a friend.
Abraham Lincoln

Pastor Michael Pitts of Cornerstone Church in Toledo, Ohio preaches one of the most enlightening sermons I've ever heard on dysfunctional relationships titled *"Get Off My Boat"* from the book of Jonah. Let's look at this passage of Scripture and see if we can glean some helpful things regarding being set free from ungodly and unhealthy friendships.

Identify Friends Who Are Running From God

Jonah 1:1-3

Underline the phrase "Jonah ran away from the Lord."

1 The word of the LORD came to Jonah son of Amittai: 2 "Go to the great city of Nineveh and preach against it, because its wickedness has come up before me." 3 But Jonah ran away from the LORD and headed for Tarshish. He went down to Joppa, where he found a ship bound for that port. After paying the fare, he went aboard and sailed for Tarshish to flee from the LORD. NIV

What did God ask Jonah to do? _____

What was Jonah's response? _____

Describe the condition of a person who is disobeying God, running away from God and fleeing from the Lord.

_____

In your own life, do you have any friends influencing, controlling or manipulating your life in any way who are also rebelling against God and His Word, backslidden or prodigal in their faith ?

_____

❧**Nugget**❧ People who are running from God are going in the wrong direction. Perhaps it's a non-believer that is running from Jesus and salvation, or maybe it's a believer who is choosing to disobey God and His Word and going their own way. Jonah was called by God to do something great, and instead of running to God in obedience, he ran away from God and ended up being detrimental to those he came in contact with.

Identify People Who Cause Storms In Your Life

1.   Jonah 1:3-4

Underline the phrases "a great wind" and "a violent storm."

3 But Jonah ran away from the LORD and headed for Tarshish. He went down to Joppa, where he found a ship bound for that port. After paying the fare, he went aboard and sailed for Tarshish to flee from the LORD. 4 Then the LORD sent a great wind on the sea, and such a violent storm arose that the ship threatened to break up. NIV

When Jonah ran from the Lord, where did he end up? _____

_____

What type of storm threatened the boat and passengers? _____

_____

Think about your life; are you facing a storm? _____

If so, reflect for a moment and identify when this storm began. Is there any connection to your storm and the relationships you have with people that are disobeying, running from or fleeing from God's presence? In other words, have you become the friendship headquarters for backsliders, sinners and rebels? Perhaps the storm that has entered your life emotionally, mentally, spiritually and even physically has a direct connection to an unhealthy, ungodly relationship in your life. Perhaps it's time to do a boat inventory.

Who's on your boat relationally? _____

Are there any people in your life that consistently create a storm for you or your family emotionally, mentally, financially, spiritually or physically?

_____

2.   Jonah 1:5-10

Underline the phrase "Jonah had gone below deck."

5 All the sailors were afraid and each cried out to his own god. And they threw the cargo into the sea to lighten the ship. But Jonah had gone below deck, where he lay down and fell into a deep sleep. 6 The captain went to him and said, "How can you sleep? Get up and call on your god! Maybe he will take notice of us, and we will not perish." 7 Then the sailors said to each other, "Come, let us cast lots to find out who is responsible for this calamity." They cast lots and the lot fell on Jonah. 8 So they asked him, "Tell us, who is responsible for making all this trouble for us? What do you do? Where do you come from? What is your country? From what people are you?" 9 He answered, "I am a Hebrew and I worship the LORD, the God of heaven, who made the sea and the land." 10 This terrified them and they asked, "What have you done?" (They knew he was running away from the LORD, because he had already told them so.) NIV

Who was responsible for the storm? _____

What was Jonah doing during the storm? _____

What were the sailors doing during the storm? _____

_____

⋙Nugget⋙ Have you ever noticed that co-dependent, dysfunctional, disobedient people on the run from God are apathetic, lethargic, asleep and unwilling to help in the midst of the storm? Have you ever noticed that other people cannot bail out the Jonahs of the world by rowing harder, spending their money and paying the price that their Jonah is not willing to pay? The boat owners were the ones using their energy, throwing their luggage and their wealth overboard, while disobedient Jonah was asleep in the bottom of the boat!

Notice that Jonah described himself as a Hebrew who worshipped the Lord of heaven. Often those who are backslidden are the most guilt-ridden, and although they know they are running from obedience to God, they may say things like, *"Well, I am a Christian and I was raised in this denomination"* or *"I go to that church,"* etc. They hope their spiritual pedigree will somehow compensate for their disobedience.

Identify The Solution For Calming The Storm

Jonah 1:11-15

Underline the phrases "What should we do to you to make the sea calm down for us?" and "Then they took Jonah and threw him overboard, and the raging sea grew calm."

"11 The sea was getting rougher and rougher. So they asked him, "What should we do to you to make the sea calm down for us?" 12 "Pick me up and throw me into the sea," he replied, "and it will become calm. I know that it is my fault that this great storm has come upon you." 13 Instead, the men did their best to row back to land. But they could not, for the sea grew even wilder than before. 14 Then they cried to the LORD, "O LORD, please do not let us die for taking this man's life. Do not hold us accountable for killing an innocent man, for you, O LORD, have done as you pleased." 15 Then they took Jonah and threw him overboard, and the raging sea grew calm." NIV

Beware the danger signals that flag problems: silence, secretiveness, or sudden outburst.
Sylvia Porter

People usually reach a breaking point in relationships, whether in marriage, friendship, with children, coworkers, employers. At some point they can't take the relational storm any more and they must make tough decisions.

In verse 11, what did the sailors ask Jonah? _____

In verse 12, what did Jonah say? _____

❧**Nugget**❧   For peace to return to our lives, it is often going to require getting certain people off our boat! Reread verse 11 and meditate on the question they asked. We may have to throw people off our physical, emotional, mental or spiritual boat in order to find peace in our lives. We can't always literally throw people off our boat and out of our lives completely, especially if they are family. However, we can deny them access to our emotions, our minds, our time, our finances and certain areas of our lives.

In verse 13, what did the sailors do? _____

Why do we think we can "fix it"? Listen, if people don't want to be fixed, you can't fix them. If they don't want to obey and follow God, you can't make them. Rowing harder, preaching at them longer, taking on more of their responsibilities, covering for them and making excuses for them will not fix them or calm your storm.

Describe the conflicted feelings the sailors were having according to verse 14.

_____

On one hand they wanted some calm back in their lives, but on the other hand they were feeling guilty about making Jonah be responsible for his decisions and his life.

How do you see this played out in modern society among friends and relatives?

_____

In verse 15, when they finally threw Jonah off their boat and ended their relationship with him, what happened for them?

_____

Is the light bulb going on? Are you feeding unhealthy relationships, staying in dysfunctional and co-dependant friendships? Is guilt or your desire to enable others causing you to be unwilling to throw Jonah off your boat? As a result, are you living a stormy life?

For your own peace of mind and heart, perhaps you need to prayerfully consider if there are any Jonah's on your boat and then seek the Lord on how to throw Jonah overboard!

Identify Healthy Relational Boundaries

You are not responsible for "Jonah's" life, success or future! That is between your Jonah and God. In the end, Jonah repented, got right with God and obeyed the Lord's will. Remember God has a plan for the Jonahs in your life, and at times it may require you to set some healthy boundaries in order for them to come to their senses and follow God's will.

Jonah 1:16-17

Underline the phrase "the Lord provided a great fish."

"16 At this the men greatly feared the LORD, and they offered a sacrifice to the LORD and made vows to him. 17 But the LORD provided a great fish to swallow Jonah, and Jonah was inside the fish three days and three nights." NIV

What happened to the sailors' relationships with God when they threw Jonah overboard?

_____

How did God take care of and provide for Jonah? _____

In the end Jonah finally repented and obeyed God's will for his life. This never would have happened if the sailors had kept Jonah on the boat. In the same way, it's our job is to throw all of our Jonah friends off our boat; our mental boat, our emotional boat, our spiritual boat and our physical boat. God is prepared to take care of Jonah, so let God do His work in the Jonahs in your life!

Seven Friends To Avoid Like The Plague

Now, let's get a closer look at some of the personality types we need to avoid like the plague!

#1.   Tilly The Troublemaker

Proverbs 16:28

Underline the word "troublemaker." Circle the word "gossips."

Troublemakers start fights; gossips break up friendships. The Message

What does this verse call those who like to start fights? _____

What type of person breaks up friendships? _____

Based on this verse, what type of people should you disassociate with? _____

_____

The troublemaker is perverse and false. They like to stir up trouble, plant deception, tell falsehoods and pervert truth. Avoid these people wherever you find them—at the office, in the neighborhood, at school, in church. Troublemakers make trouble for you and everyone around them. Don't give troublemakers access to your boat.

#2.   Penelope The Pretend Friend

Proverbs 18:24

Underline the phrase "pretend to be friends."

There are "friends" who pretend to be friends, but there is a friend who sticks closer than a brother. TLB

Pretend friends are also known as "convenient friends" and "fair-weather friends." They are there when friendship is convenient or in their best interest, but when the chips are down, they aren't around.

Describe a "pretend" friend. _____

Describe a "real" friend. _____

_____

#3.   Hilda The Hot Head

Proverbs 22:24-25

Underline the phrase "friends with a hot-tempered man."

24 Do not make friends with a hot-tempered man, do not associate with one easily angered, 25 or you may learn his ways and get yourself ensnared. NIV

What kind of friendship are we to have with hot-tempered or angry people?

_____

Why?_____

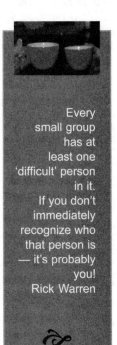

Every small group has at least one 'difficult' person in it. If you don't immediately recognize who that person is — it's probably you!
Rick Warren

Hot heads are everywhere: at the grocery store, your child's basketball or hockey game, driving cars, in line, at work and any place that a little patience is required. It's true, you become like those you hang around. Friends with a short fuse will eventually burn you. Hot heads and their tempers are contentious, contagious and infectious. Steer clear. Give them a big *"Heave, ho, off my boat you go!"*

#4.   Gertrude The Gossip

Psalm 101:4-6

Underline the phrase "put a gag on the gossip."

4 The crooked in heart keep their distance; I refuse to shake hands with those who plan evil. 5 I put a gag on the gossip who bad-mouths his neighbor; I can't stand arrogance. 6 But I have my eye on salt-of-the-earth people—they're the ones I want working with me; Men and women on the straight and narrow—these are the ones I want at my side. The Message

According to verse 4, who do we refuse to be friends with? *Those crooked in heart and those who plan evil.*

According to verse 5, what do we gag and not tolerate? *Gossip*

Gossip: What is gossip? Gossip is also translated as "talebearer," comes from the Hebrew word "nirgan" and its meaning includes: to murmur, to complain, to whisper, being a backbiter, a talebearer, to slander.[2]

According to verse 6, what type of friends do we want? *Those on the straight and narrow*

Gossips create fires. Their murmuring, complaining, backbiting, slandering, whispers, embellishments, untruths and half-the-story lies break up friendships, hurt reputations and destroy people's lives. Proverbs 26:20 tells us, *"When you run out of wood, the fire goes out; when the gossip ends, the quarrel dies down." The Message* Don't add wood to the gossip's bonfire and the fire will go out.

If you've gotten in the bad habit of being "gossipy," just remember that gossips are not your friends because what they gossip about regarding other people in your presence, they will gossip about regarding you to others when you are not present. Don't be a gossip. Throw gossips off the boat of your life.

#5.   Helga The Hell Raiser

Proverbs 1:10-15

Underline the phrase "raise some hell."

10 Dear friend, if bad companions tempt you, don't go along with them. 11 If they say—"Let's go out and raise some hell. Let's beat up some old man, mug some old woman. 12 Let's pick them clean and get them ready for their funerals. 13 We'll load up on top-quality loot. We'll haul it home by the truckload. 14 Join us for the time of your life! With us, it's share and share alike!"—15 Oh, friend, don't give them a second look; don't listen to them for a minute. The Message

Our choice of friends begins at an early age, and is important at every season of life. Those we associate with have the potential to enrich or destroy our lives.

Describe this social group. _____

This passage describes the ungodly partiers, the mischievous, the rowdies, the vandals and the criminal. Don't be too quick to stereotype these types of people. It's not just the *"classic trailer-trash, wife-beater, gang-bang, prison-types"* that make up this group. You can find them in the popular *"country-clubbing, martini-sipping, cigar-bar adultery crowd"* just as often. The issue isn't your economic status, but the status of your heart's desire to live over the edge.

Have you had opportunities to hang with the wrong crowd? _____

What key decisions did you make to avoid going in the wrong direction? _____

In verse 15, what type of relationship does God want us to have with these types of people?

_____

#6. Gretta The God-Rejecter

2 Corinthians 6:14-15

Underline the phrase "those who reject God."

14 Don't become partners with <u>those who reject God.</u> How can you make a partnership out of right and wrong? That's not partnership; that's war. Is light best friends with dark? 15 Does Christ go strolling with the Devil? Do trust and mistrust hold hands? The Message

We don't become friends with whom? _____

How can you be in the world and not of the world; befriending sinners like Jesus did, without becoming like those who reject God?

_____

_____

We are to let our lights shine before men, and we are to become all things to all men so that by all means we may lead them to Christ. We are to be a witness to those in darkness, but we are not to become best friends, partners or "yoked together" with unbelievers and those who reject God. A great passage on this balance is found in 1 Corinthians 9:19-22. There's a very good reason for living this way, which we will look at in the next verse of Scripture.

#7.   Bertha and Her Bad Company

1 Corinthians 15:33

Underline the phrase "bad company."

Do not be misled: "<u>Bad company</u> corrupts good character." NIV

This is the bottom line. What do bad friends do to you? <u>*Corrupt my good character*</u>

I have a hard time believing that one of my favorite 8-tracks (for those of you that never heard of an 8-track, it was the CD of the '70s!) in high school, before I came to know Christ, was by a group called, "Bad Company." Isn't that pitiful? Bad company is bad news. The friends we associate with are a huge, huge, huge issue in terms of our own Christian life. We are either being influenced or we are being influencers, and when our primary friends do not share our faith in Jesus and our love for God and His Word, there is a good chance that their influence will have a negative affect on our own character.

Think about other 'bad company"—people who whine, complain, are moody, negative and downers. Be careful that their company doesn't corrupt your good character!

&**Nugget**& One final thought: as parents, we spend years training, nurturing and protecting our children. We do our best to instill godly values and good character in our children, and yet one wrong friend can corrupt our children. How important is it that we pay attention to the friends our kids hang out with?

I hope you've been challenged and stirred up to review some of the friendships in your life. I pray that you will prayerfully consider the boundaries you need to set and when necessary throw some people off your boat.

> Associate yourself with men of good quality if you esteem your own reputation, for 'tis better to be alone than in bad company.
> George Washington

&

Scriptures To Chew On

Taking time to meditate on and memorize God's Word is invaluable. Hiding His Word in our hearts will strengthen us for the present and arm us for the future. Here are two verses to memorize and chew on this week. Write these verses on index cards and carry them with you this week. If you will post them in your bathroom, dashboard, desk, locker or other convenient places, you will find these Scriptures taking root in your heart.

"Do not be misled:
Bad company corrupts good character."
1 Corinthians 15:33, NIV

"Do not make friends with a hot-tempered man,
do not associate with one easily angered,
or you may learn his ways and get yourself ensnared."
Proverbs 22:24-25, NIV

Group Discussion

1.   Describe your experience with a Jonah and the storm you faced.

2.   Describe how you handled the internal conflict or "guilt trip" as you threw your Jonah off the boat.

3.   Which one of the 7 Friends To Avoid Like The Plague do you find the most challenging in your own life?

---

[1]Cloud, Henry and John Townsend. Boundaries. Grand Rapids: Zondervan, 1992.
[2]The Online Bible Thayer's Greek Lexicon and Brown Driver & Briggs Hebrew Lexicon, Copyright (c)1993, Woodside Bible Fellowship, Ontario, Canada. Licensed from the Institute for Creation Research.

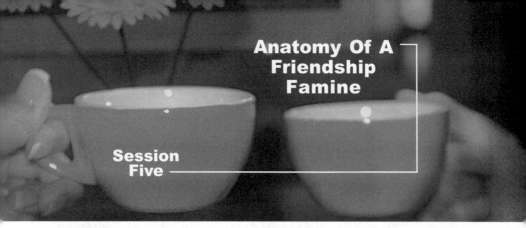

Three Dog Night had it right, *"One is the loneliest number . . ."* God said it in the beginning: "It's not good for man to be alone." We weren't created to be an island. Sure, Simon and Garfunkel sang, *"I am a rock, I am an island . . ."* but it's not true! No man is an island, to quote the Renaissance era poet and clergyman, John Donne.

The writer of Ecclesiastes understood a relational truth. *"I turned my head and saw yet another wisp of smoke on its way to nothingness: a solitary person, completely alone — no children, no family, no friends — yet working obsessively late into the night, compulsively greedy for more and more, never bothering to ask, "Why am I working like a dog, never having any fun? And who cares?" More smoke. A bad business. It's better to have a partner than go it alone. Share the work, share the wealth. And if one falls down, the other helps, but if there's no one to help, tough! Two in a bed warm each other. Alone, you shiver all night. By yourself you're unprotected. With a friend you can face the worst. Can you round up a third? A three-stranded rope isn't easily snapped." Ecclesiastes 4:7-12, The Message*

Life is meant to be shared. Sure, you can be a workaholic, a hermit or a loner, but that is not God's best. He wants your life relationally rich! He'll knit you together with others and most importantly, with Him. God promises to set the solitary in families. If you are single, alone or lonely, God wants you to be relationally rich and He has a plan for helping you reap the blessing of rich friendships.

> There are two kinds of people in the world— those who walk into a room and say, 'There you are'— and those who say, 'Here I am!'
> Abigail Van Buren

If you are feeling relationally challenged, alone or discouraged, don't despair. None of us have done the friendship-thing perfectly. As I've already shared, I sowed a 13 year "friendship famine" in my own life. I know what it's like to look around and say, *"Hey, what happened to all my friends? All I see are my four toddlers, diapers, bottles, strollers and Legos!"* I was in that busy season of mom-hood with preschoolers, and didn't even have time for meaningful friendships. I didn't sow friendship seeds and I didn't reap friends. Pretty plain, isn't it?

If you're experiencing a friendship famine, the good news is that your barren friendship field can grow! But first, let's look at the "bad news."

➷**Nugget**➷ If I don't have a plethora of friends, is there a reason? We need to be honest with ourselves and with God. Is my friendship famine simply the result of my not sowing any friendship seeds or am I doing something to undermine potential friendships? Am I doing anything that would cause friends to avoid, diss or run from me? Am I being an irritant? Self-absorbed? Critical? A stick in the mud? Boring? A whiner? A drag? A big pain in the drain? Face it, no one wants to be around a boring downer or the person having a constant pity party. Are you making yourself enjoyable to be around? A pleasure to work with? Easy to talk to? We have a responsibility to be the type of friend that exhibits godly qualities that people enjoy being around. If you identify areas of weakness in your own friendship quotient, seek the Lord and adjust. Now, let's look at the good news!

If You Want To Have Friends, Sow Friendliness

Are you looking for a big harvest of friendship? If you've experienced famine in your relationships, it's time to sow and reap. Are you ready to plant a bag of "friendship seeds"? It's easier than you think.

Let's look at the law of seedtime and harvest that God has established.

1. Genesis 8:22

   Underline the phrase "seedtime and harvest."

   While the earth remains, <u>seedtime and harvest,</u> cold and heat, winter and summer, and day and night shall not cease. NKJV

   What four things did God say would not cease?

   Cold (Winter)   _Day_

   Hot (Summer)   _Night_

2. Genesis 26:1, 12-14

   Underline the words "famine," "Isaac planted" and "the same year reaped."

   1 Now there was a famine in the land . . . 12 Isaac planted crops in that land and the same year reaped a hundredfold, because the LORD blessed him. 13 The man became rich, and his wealth continued to grow until he became very wealthy. 14 He had so many flocks and herds and servants that the Philistines envied him. NIV

   In verse 1, what was Isaac experiencing? _famine_

   In verse 12, what did Isaac do in the midst of a famine? _Planted crops_

   In verses 12-14, what happened to Isaac? _The Lord blessed him, and he became wealthy_

   Do you believe that if you sow "friendship crops" in the midst of a friendship famine, God will cause you to reap and become very rich and wealthy in relationships? _Yes._

3. Galatians 6:7-10

    Underline the sentence "What a person plants, he will harvest."

    *7 Don't be misled: No one makes a fool of God. What a person plants,
    he will harvest. The person who plants selfishness, ignoring the needs
    of others—ignoring God—8 harvests a crop of weeds. All he'll have to
    show for his life is weeds! But the one who plants in response to God,
    letting God's Spirit do the growth work in him, harvests a crop of real
    life, eternal life. 9 So let's not allow ourselves to get fatigued doing
    good. At the right time we will harvest a good crop if we don't give up,
    or quit. The Message*

    If we plant selfishness, what do we reap? __Weeds__

    If we plant godly seeds, what do we reap? __Real life - eternal life__

    What does verse 9 tell us about patience? __Not to give up or
    quit if we want to harvest a good crop__

4. Proverbs 18:24

    Underline the phrase "be friendly."

    *A man who has friends must himself be friendly, but there is a friend
    who sticks closer than a brother. NKJV*

    If you want to have friends, what must you be? __friendly__

    How can you sow "friendliness" into the people in your life? __By being
    a good friend. Be kind and listen__

    Sometimes, all it takes is little things like smiling, saying hello, asking
    questions and taking the initiative to show you are genuinely interested
    in others.

↝**Nugget**↝ If you want a friendship harvest you will have to take the initiative. If you've ever attended church, gone to the neighborhood cookout or the office party and left feeling like "no one was friendly" at the event, it's time to take a look in the mirror! Don't put the responsibility for your friendship harvest on the shoulders of others; don't expect them to reach out and include you unless you are willing to reach out first and take the initiative in being friendly. If you sit back and wait for others to come up to you, to include you, to get to know you or become your best friend, you may wait a long time.

Perhaps you feel insecure in reaching out or in planting friendship seeds. How do you break the friendship famine cycle? Here are some seeds you can begin to plant into the lives of those around you.

Plant Seeds of Genuine Interest In Others

Sow interest! Be interested.

As Dale Carnegie once said, *"You can make more friends in two months by becoming interested in other people than you can in two years of trying to get other people interested in you."*[1] I believe this is the most misunderstood secret to mutually enjoyable personal relationships. Think about it. When was the last time you took note of the affairs, challenges, projects, dreams, events and dynamics of the people in your world and asked them a meaningful question about their life? And . . . then continued to show interest in their lives by asking several good follow-up questions?

The most basic of all human needs is the need to understand and be understood. The best way to understand people is to listen to them.
Ralph Nichols

If this type of conversation has not taken place in a long time, you are sowing a friendship famine. If your most recent conversations with family, friends or co-workers have revolved around you telling them stories about you, you might want to do a 180 and start asking questions that show you're interested in them. Being interested in others goes against our selfish nature, so remember, the key to being interesting is to be interested!

Showing disinterest in someone is worse than showing dislike. Dislike says, "I just don't like you." Disinterest says, "I don't care about you." Being ignored is worse than being insulted. Ignoring someone says, "You don't exist." Insulting someone says, "You exist and here are your flaws." If you avoid others, you are telling them, "I notice you, and I don't want to be near you." If you are indifferent toward others, you are saying, "You don't impress me in any way. You are nothing to me." Which is worse? They all speak friendship famine!

If we sow interest in others in an atmosphere of love and acceptance, we'll find a whole new level of rich relationships opens up to us. Let's see what God's Word has to say about this.

1.   Philippians 2:19-22

        Underline the way Timothy sowed acceptance into the lives of the Philippians.

        19 But I hope and trust in the Lord Jesus soon to send Timothy to you, so that I may also be encouraged and cheered by learning news of you. 20 For I have no one like him [no one of so kindred a spirit] who will be so <u>genuinely interested in your welfare and devoted to your interests.</u> 21 For the others all seek [to advance] their own interests, not those of Jesus Christ (the Messiah). 22 But Timothy's tested worth you know, how as a son with his father he has toiled with me zealously in [serving and helping to advance] the good news (the Gospel). AMP

        The Living Bible says it this way:

        20 There is no one like Timothy for having a real interest in you; 21 everyone else seems to be worrying about his own plans and not those of Jesus Christ.

        According to verse 20, what made Timothy stand out? *His real Interest in others.*

        Are people like Timothy hard to find or commonplace? *Hard to find*

What was Timothy truly interested in? _Jesus Christ_

What were others interested in? _Their own plans._

In what ways could you be more like Timothy to the people in your life?

Make more time for them, spend quality time with them, Be a better listener.

2.   Philippians 2:4

Underline the word that describes our approach with others.

"Don't just think about your own affairs, but be interested in others, too, and in what they are doing. TLB

What does this tell us concerning our interest in our own lives? _____

We're self absorbed

What part of others' lives are we to be interested in? _What they are doing_

The way to show interest is simply asking questions. When you ask others questions about themselves and the things they are doing—their hobbies, their dreams and goals—it demonstrates that you genuinely care.

3.   John 16:5-6

Underline the thing that Jesus rebuked.

5 But now I am going away to the one who sent me; and none of you seems interested in the purpose of my going; none wonders why. 6 Instead you are only filled with sorrow. TLB

What were the disciples not interested in? _The purpose of His going_

What consumed their interest? *Their sorrow*

In what ways are we often consumed with our own "pity parties" and not aware of the interests of those around us?

_____

4.   Zechariah 7:6

Underline the thing that God is interested in.

And when you held feasts, was that for me? Hardly. You're interested in religion, I'm interested in people. The Message

What's the bottom line on what God is interested in? _____

_____

When you and I show an interest in others, we are acting like God. We stand out, because as the Apostle Paul said there are not many people like Timothy who will naturally care for the interests of others. Let's be the kind of people that overcome our own needs by sowing into the lives of others.

As a result, we will reap a harvest!

Plant Seeds Of Transparency And Vulnerability

Most people want to feel noticed, liked, accepted, appreciated and approved of by the people important to them. We want people to want us. We have a need to know and be known. Secular behavior and motivation experts like Abraham Maslow teach us that self-disclosure is a basic need of human beings. Once certain basic needs are met in a person's life, they have a need to disclose personal information as this creates a feeling of closeness between people.

I like what Christian author and founder of the Family Dynamics Institute, Joe Beam, said in his article "Becoming Vulnerable", (http://www.familydynamics.net, used by permission of the author):

"Removing all masks to let another see who we really are ('warts and all') means risking everything in that relationship. If the other person doesn't accept us when they encounter our undisguised selves, we feel absolute rejection. We likely won't continue the relationship, even if the other person wants to, because we know that he or she has seen the true us and been repulsed by the discovery. So how do we grow past that fear and decide to reveal our true selves? We do it in stages. We start by sharing facts that are non-threatening; facts that we feel won't be reacted to negatively. As we share those innocuous facts of our lives (e.g. "I was born in the USA,") we register every reaction of the person to whom we share. Any lack of interest or hint of displeasure on their part causes us to stop the process. We're certainly not going to reveal potentially threatening facts (e.g. "When I was a kid I was arrested,") if we note any disinterest or rejection as we share innocuous facts. On the other hand, as we register interest and acceptance we tend to reveal more threatening facts. We can become so trusting of the seemingly unconditional acceptance of the other person that we tell him or her things about ourselves we've never told anyone."

The Apostle Paul was good at sharing his heart, being vulnerable with others and planting these types of seeds into the lives of others. Let's see what we can learn about sowing vulnerability and transparency seeds.

1.   2 Corinthians 6:11-13

        Underline the way Paul was vulnerable.

        11 We have spoken freely to you, Corinthians, and opened wide our hearts to you. 12 We are not withholding our affection from you, but you

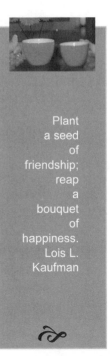

Plant a seed of friendship; reap a bouquet of happiness.
Lois L. Kaufman

are withholding yours from us. 13 As a fair exchange-I speak as to my children-open wide your hearts also. NIV

11 Oh, my dear Corinthian friends! I have told you all my feelings; I love you with all my heart. 12 Any coldness still between us is not because of any lack of love on my part but because your love is too small and does not reach out to me and draw me in. 13 I am talking to you now as if you truly were my very own children. Open your hearts to us! Return our love! TLB

How did Paul communicate? _____

How does this passage describe self-disclosure on Paul's part? _____

_____

What does Paul encourage the believers to do? _____

_____

2.　　1 Thessalonians 2:8

Underline the things that Paul shares with the believers.

We loved you so much that we were delighted to share with you not only the gospel of God but our lives as well, because you had become so dear to us. NIV

How did Paul describe his feelings for these believers? _____

In your relationships, do you share both the gospel and your own life?

_____

I hope this lesson has inspired and encouraged you to reach out to others. Get ready for a rich harvest of God-knit friendships as you sow friendship seeds!

Scriptures To Chew On

Taking time to meditate on and memorize God's Word is invaluable. Hiding His Word in our hearts will strengthen us for the present and arm us for the future. Here are two verses to memorize and chew on this week. Write these verses on index cards and carry them with you this week. If you will post them in your bathroom, dashboard, desk, locker or other convenient places, you will find these Scriptures taking root in your heart.

> *"So this is my prayer: that your love will flourish and that you will not only love much but well. Learn to love appropriately.*
> *You need to use your head and test your feelings so that your love is sincere and intelligent, not sentimental gush. Live a lover's life, circumspect and exemplary, a life Jesus will be proud of: bountiful in fruits from the soul, making Jesus Christ attractive to all, getting everyone involved in the glory and praise of God."*
> *Philippians 1:9-11, The Message*

> *"Don't be misled: No one makes a fool of God.*
> *What a person plants, he will harvest.*
> *The person who plants selfishness, ignoring the needs of others—ignoring God!—harvests a crop of weeds. All he'll have to show for his life is weeds! But the one who plants in response to God, letting God's Spirit do the growth work in him, harvests a crop of real life, eternal life. So let's not allow ourselves to get fatigued doing good.*
> *At the right time we will harvest*
> *a good crop if we don't give up, or quit."*
> *Galatians 6:7-9. The Message*

Group Discussion

1. Describe the law of sowing and reaping in areas of your life. What role does the seed, soil and patience play?

2. Describe the power of showing interest in others. Share a story of someone showing interest in your life.

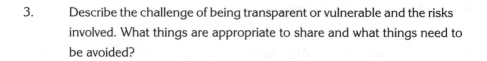

3.   Describe the challenge of being transparent or vulnerable and the risks involved. What things are appropriate to share and what things need to be avoided?

[1] Carnegie, Dale. How to Win Friends and Influence People. New York: Pocket Books, 1990.

A Friend Of God

God is looking for friends! Did you know that? You may have a wonderful husband, children you love and cherish, the dearest chick friends in the world and a God-knit Jonathan-David friendship, but there is still likely going to be a place inside of you that longs for Someone to know and understand the deepest part of you. The Bible says, *"Deep calls to deep,"* which means the deepest part of us is calling out and only a deep friendship with God can answer back. All the human friendships God sends us are simply the "icing on the cake," but He's the cake! Yes, He's the cake! So, let's end this study on friendship by talking about the Friendship that matters most: being a Friend of God.

Many people have recognized this! Blaise Pascal, the French mathematician and physicist said, *"There is a God-shaped vacuum in the heart of every person and it can never be filled by any created thing. It can only be filled by God, made known through Jesus Christ."* It's true. The Christian artists, Plumb, sang a song about a God-shaped hole in all of us, and the movie *Bruce Almighty* made it famous: *"There's a God-shaped hole in all of us and the restless soul is searching . . ."* It's true! There's a popular worship song titled, *Friend of God* written by Israel Houghton that goes like this,

> *Is it true that you are mindful of me?*
> *That you hear me when I call?*
> *And is it true that you are thinking of me*
> *How you love me,*
> *It's amazing . . .*
> *I am a friend of God*
> *He calls me friend.*

If you make a great deal of Christ, He will make a great deal of you; but if you make but a little of Christ, Christ will make but a little of you.
R.A. Torrey

God Almighty, Lord of Glory.
You have called me friend.
I am a Friend of God.
He calls me Friend.

It's something to ponder, isn't it? When we confess Him as Lord, Jesus calls us friends. Think about that. How well do we know Him as our Friend?

❧**Nugget**❧ Like many people, I have had great respect for Oprah; but I am not her friend. I've read a few articles and biographies about Oprah, and although I know some things about her, I do not know her personally. I've found that many people have this type of relationship with God. They have great respect for God. They've read a few books and maybe even a bit of the Bible. They know some things about God, but they do not know Him personally. Let's see what the Bible says about how we can get to know God the Father, Jesus the Son and the Holy Spirit personally.

You Can Be God's Friend

Perhaps you're a believer and Jesus is your Lord and Savior, but do you also know Him as your Friend? You can. If you're not a believer, I'd like to encourage you to re-read the introductory section titled "First Things First," invite Him into your life and begin a brilliant new friendship with God.

Let's begin our study by looking at what the Bible says about being God's friend.

1.   Psalm 25:14

Underline the phrase "friendship with God."

Friendship with God is reserved for those who reverence him. With them alone he shares the secrets of his promises. TLB

Who gets to be God's friend? _Those who reverence Him_

What does God share with His friends? _the secrets of His promise._

Listen to how the Message Bible relays this verse:

God-friendship is for God-worshipers; they are the ones he confides in.

How would you describe the components of being God's friend?

Open heart

2. Psalm 34:15

    Underline the phrase "his friends."

    God keeps an eye on his friends, his ears pick up every moan and groan. The Message

    What does God do for His friends? Keeps an eye on them

    It's nice to know we have friends in high places! We're never alone.

3. Micah 7:5-7

    Underline the friends you potentially cannot trust and the friend you can always count on.

    5 Don't trust your neighbor, don't confide in your friend. Watch your words, even with your spouse. 6 Neighborhoods and families are falling to pieces. The closer they are — sons, daughters, in-laws — the worse they can be. Your own family is the enemy. 7 But me, I'm not giving up. I'm sticking around to see what GOD will do. I'm waiting for God to make things right. I'm counting on God to listen to me. The Message

    ∂•**Nugget**∂• People are going to let you down; God has designed it that way. There are times when even our best friend, husband and family disappoint us, intentionally or unintentionally. No human being is designed to be our "all in all."

When every human friend you have has let you down, what Friend can you count on and why?

God!!

3.   Romans 5:9-11

Underline the phrase "this amazing friendship with God."

9 Now that we are set right with God by means of this sacrificial death, the consummate blood sacrifice, there is no longer a question of being at odds with God in any way. 10 If, when we were at our worst, we were put on friendly terms with God by the sacrificial death of his Son, now that we're at our best, just think of how our lives will expand and deepen by means of his resurrection life! 11 Now that we have actually received this amazing friendship with God, we are no longer content to simply say it in plodding prose. We sing and shout our praises to God through Jesus, the Messiah! The Message

According to verses 9-10, what has happened to our friendship with God as a result of Jesus' death on the cross?

According to verse 11, what does being a friend of God inspire our hearts to do?

Sing and shout our praises

⋙**Nugget**⋙ When we have a personal relationship with God through Jesus Christ, when His friendship is real to us and not just a religious duty, we can't help but talk about Him! Think about your love life. If you're married, did you keep it a big secret when you fell in love with your husband? No! You light up when you think about your husband. You want to "show him off" to all your girlfriends, right? You want to tell everyone what a hunk your husband is, how caring, smart, funny he is. If that is the natural response in our most loving human relationships, why do we get so dull when it comes to our friendship with God Almighty?

4.   2 Corinthians 13:14

Underline the phrases "amazing grace," "extravagant love" and "intimate friendship."

The amazing grace of the Master, Jesus Christ, the extravagant love of God, the intimate friendship of the Holy Spirit, be with all of you. The Message

Isn't it wonderful to know that we can have a personal friendship with each person in the Godhead—God the Father, Jesus the Master, and the Holy Spirit?

What does our friendship with the Master, Jesus, bring to our lives?

_____

_____

What does our friendship with God, the Father, fill us with?

_____

_____

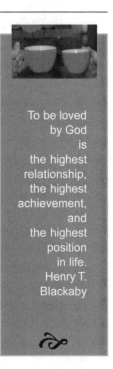

To be loved by God is the highest relationship, the highest achievement, and the highest position in life.
Henry T. Blackaby

What does our friendship with the Holy Spirit look like?

_____

_____

Abraham Was God's Friend

1.   James 2:23

Underline the phrase "the friend of God."

And so it happened just as the Scriptures say: "Abraham believed God, so God declared him to be righteous." He was even called "the friend of God." NLT

According to this verse, what was Abraham called?

the friend of God

What caused Abraham to be called "the friend of God"?

Abraham believed God.

Simple, right? Faith pleases God. Though we haven't seen Him, we love Him and He calls us friend. Our friendship with God begins with belief.

Do you believe God? *yes*

Do you take Him at His Word? *yes*

Describe a time when you had to choose between believing God and His Word rather than your own thoughts, circumstances or the words of others.

_____

_____

2.   Genesis 18:19

Underline the phrase "Yes, I've settled on him."

Yes, I've settled on him as the one to train his children and future family to observe GOD's way of life, live kindly and generously and fairly, so that GOD can complete in Abraham what he promised him. The Message

Here, we get a little more insight into what God liked about Abraham, his friend.

What qualities did God see in Abraham? _____

_____

What role does trust play in a friendship? _____

Can God trust you to keep His Word? _____

Do you trust God to perform His Word? _____

3.   Isaiah 41:8

Underline the phrase "he was my friend."

But as for you, O Israel, you are mine, my chosen ones; for you are Abraham's family, and he was my friend. TLB

It's nice being related to people who are friends with God! Through our faith in Jesus Christ, the Bible says we've become part of Abraham's family and heirs of all that God promised him. *"So those now who live by faith are blessed along with Abraham, who lived by faith — this is no new doctrine!" Galatians 3:9-10, The Message*

Since we are related to Abraham through Jesus Christ, what does God call us?

His friend

If you study Abraham's life you will find that because of his friendship with God, also known as a covenant, everything that belonged to Abraham was God's and everything that belonged to God was Abraham's. Who do you think got the better deal?

Moses Was God's Friend

1.   Exodus 33:11

Underline the phrase "his friend."

So the LORD spoke to Moses face to face, as a man speaks to his friend. NKJV

How did God speak with Moses? *face to face*

2.   Exodus 33:14-19

Underline the word "Presence" and the phrase "I am pleased with you and I know you by name."

14 The LORD replied, "My Presence will go with you, and I will give you rest." 15 Then Moses said to him, "If your Presence does not go with us, do not send us up from here. 16 How will anyone know that you are pleased with me and with your people unless you go with us? What else will distinguish me and your people from all the other people on the face of the earth?" 17 And the LORD said to Moses, "I will do the very thing you have asked, because I am pleased with you and I know you by name." 18 Then Moses said, "Now show me your glory." 19 And the LORD said, "I will cause all my goodness to pass in front of you, and I will proclaim my name, the LORD, in your presence. I will have mercy on whom I will have mercy, and I will have compassion on whom I will have compassion. NIV

I love this passage. The reality of God's Presence and friendship can and should be tangible in our lives.

I am not lost, I'm wandering in God's grace.

In verses 15 and 18, what did Moses say he couldn't live without? _____

_____

In verse 16, what did Moses say that God's Presence demonstrated? _____

_____

In verses 14, 17 and 19, the Lord speaks very personally to Moses.

What did God say?

_____

_____

_____

How does the thought that God would know your name impact you?

_____

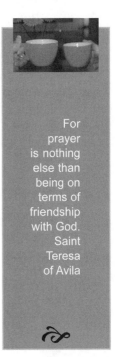

How would you describe the idea of having God's Presence in your life?

_____

_____

For prayer is nothing else than being on terms of friendship with God.
Saint Teresa of Avila

3.   Exodus 34:5-7

Underline the phrase "the Lord came down."

5 Then the LORD came down in the cloud and stood there with him and proclaimed his name, the LORD. 6 And he passed in front of Moses, proclaiming, "The LORD, the LORD, the compassionate and gracious God, slow to anger, abounding in love and faithfulness, 7 maintaining love to thousands, and forgiving wickedness, rebellion and sin. NIV

When God's Presence, goodness and friendship were tangibly manifested to Moses, what character traits did the Lord reveal about the type of God and friend He is?

Slow to anger, abounding in love + faithfulness, maintaining love to thousands, and forgiving wickedness, rebellion and sin.

Enoch Was A Friend Of God

1.   Genesis 5:22-24

Underline the phrase "Enoch walked with God."

22 And after he became the father of Methuselah, Enoch walked with God 300 years and had other sons and daughters. 23 Altogether, Enoch lived 365 years. 24 Enoch walked with God; then he was no more, because God took him away. NIV

It's hard to grasp the reality that people lived to be 365 years old!

What did Enoch do during his 300+ years? *He walked with God.*

In your own words, what does it mean to "walk with God"? *to be faithful have complete and full trust in God.*

2.   Hebrews 11:5

Underline the phrase "he pleased God."

By an act of faith, Enoch skipped death completely. "They looked all over and couldn't find him because God had taken him." We know on the basis of reliable testimony that before he was taken "he pleased God." The Message

God was pleased with Enoch. They walked together for hundreds of years. They had a rich history of friendship during Enoch's life.

Can you imagine? Enoch and the Lord were so close, God didn't want to spend another day with Enoch living on earth and God living in heaven. So God sent "Two Angels and a Chariot" and transferred Enoch to heaven, without facing death!

What did God do to Enoch? _____

What event does that sound like? _____

Jesus Calls You His Friend

1.   Proverbs 18:24

Underline the words "friends" and "friendly."

A man who has friends must himself be friendly, but there is a friend who sticks closer than a brother. NKJV

Who is the Friend that sticks closer than a brother? _*God*_____

What does that mean to you? _____

_____

2.   Luke 12:31-32

Underline the phrase "You're my dearest friends."

31 Steep yourself in God-reality, God-initiative, God-provisions. You'll find all your everyday human concerns will be met. 32 Don't be afraid of missing out. You're my dearest friends! The Father wants to give you the very kingdom itself. The Message

In verse 32, what does Jesus call those who believe and follow Him?

_____

In your own words, what does a friendship with Jesus look like?

_____

In verse 31, what does He tell His friends to do? _____

ॐ**Nugget**ॐ Can you see that Jesus isn't talking about a casual friendship? He's talking about "steeping" yourself, saturating and marinating your life with God realities! The Lord wants a close, intense and dynamic friendship with His people.

3.   John 15:12-15

Underline the phrase "I have called you friends."

12 My command is this: Love each other as I have loved you. 13 Greater love has no one than this, that he lay down his life for his friends. 14 You are my friends if you do what I command. 15 I no longer call you servants, because a servant does not know his master's business. Instead, I have called you friends, for everything that I learned from my Father I have made known to you. NIV

In verses 14 and 15, what does Jesus call His followers? _____

_____

In verse 13, what did Jesus say was the greatest thing a person can do for a friend?

_____

Jesus proved His love for us when He laid down His life on the cross.

In verse 12, what does Jesus want us to do to others? _____

_____

While we call Him Lord, Savior and Master, He calls us His friends.

Don't Fake It

Let's end this study with a dose of reality. When it comes to friendship with God, don't fake it. Don't be a phony, religious person; have the real McCoy, the genuine article. Be authentic and honest. It doesn't take long in Christian circles to learn the lingo and play pretend "churchianity." You know the drill . . . the church face on Sunday, but strife, gossip, jealousy, partying, lying, stinginess, selfishness, pride, adultery and hypocrisy the rest of the week. God's looking for real friends; those who really get it and those who really want Him. Are you one of those people?

1.   Psalm 50:16-23

      Underline the phrases "talking like we are good friends" and "it's the praising life that honors me."

      16 Next, God calls up the wicked: "What are you up to, quoting my laws, talking like we are good friends? 17 You never answer the door when I call; you treat my words like garbage. 18 If you find a thief, you make him your buddy; adulterers are your friends of choice. 19 Your

A man with God is always in the majority. John Knox

mouth drools filth; lying is a serious art form with you. 20 You stab your own brother in the back, rip off your little sister. 21 I kept a quiet patience while you did these things; you thought I went along with your game. I'm calling you on the carpet, now, laying your wickedness out in plain sight. 22 Time's up for playing fast and loose with me. I'm ready to pass sentence, and there's no help in sight! 23 It's the praising life that honors me. As soon as you set your foot on the Way, I'll show you my salvation. The Message

In verse 16, what did God say about these religious fakes? _____

_____

In verse 17, how did God describe His relationship with these phonies; what did they do with Him and His Word?

_____

In verses 18-20, what did God know about these people? _____

_____

In verses 21-22, God's patience with these people was up. What did God say?

_____

In verse 23, what type of friend is God looking for? _____

_____

2.   James 4:4

Underline the phrases "friendship with the world" and "friend of the world."

You adulterous people, don't you know that friendship with the world is hatred toward God? Anyone who chooses to be a friend of the world becomes an enemy of God. NIV

We get to choose: friendship with the world or friendship with God.

How would you describe friendship with the world? _____

_____

If we choose friendship with the world rather than friendship with God, what do we become?

_____

How would you describe friendship with God? _____

If we choose friendship with the world (the rule of lust and pride, according to 1 John 2:15-17), what does that say about our relationship with God?

_____

☙**Nugget**☙ God loves the world so much He sent His Son to die on the cross! At the same time, friendship with the world is rebuked because it takes the place reserved for the Lord alone. Friendship with the world is described in 1 John 2:15-17, *"Stop loving this evil world and all that it offers you, for when you love the world, you show that you do not have the love of the Father in you. For the world offers only the lust for physical pleasure, the lust for everything we see, and pride in our possessions. These are not from the Father. They are from this evil world. And this world is fading away, along with everything it craves. But if you do the will of God, you will live forever. NLT* Notice friendship with the world or friendship with God is something that we get to choose. God will not force Himself on us, but He gives us a free will to choose.

Are you a friend of God? I hope so. Perhaps, as you've looked at this lesson you realize that although you know some things **about** God, you do not know Him personally. If that's you, today is the day that can change! I think by now you've seen that God is looking for those who want a genuine relationship with Him. He wants to call you friend. You can begin a vital, dynamic relationship with God, through Jesus Christ, by simply turning from your sins and inviting Jesus into your life. Pray this prayer to begin your friendship with God:

"Dear God, I humble my heart before You. I want to turn from a sinful life and turn to You. Jesus, I invite You to be the Lord of my life, to forgive and cleanse me from every sin I've committed. I want to know You. I want a real, genuine friendship with You. Help me to walk with You every day. In Jesus' Name. Amen."

Scriptures To Chew On

Taking time to meditate on and memorize God's Word is invaluable. Hiding His Word in our hearts will strengthen us for the present and arm us for the future. Here are two verses to memorize and chew on this week. Write these verses on index cards and carry them with you this week. If you will post them in your bathroom, dashboard, desk, locker or other convenient places, you will find these Scriptures taking root in your heart.

"A man who has friends must himself be friendly,
But there is a friend who sticks closer than a brother."
Proverbs 18:24, NKJV

"Friendship with the LORD is reserved for those who fear him.
With them he shares the secrets of his covenant."
Psalm 25:14, NLT

Group Discussion

1. Which of these words describes the way you have viewed God?

    - Angry Distant God   - Spiritual "Santa Claus" - Mean Judge
    - Grandfather Figure   - Impersonal Force   - Genuine Friend
    - God Who Winks At Sin - Loving Father   - Merciful Forgiver

2. Describe the difference between knowing "about" someone and "knowing" someone personally.

3. Describe any changes you intend to make in your life to cultivate your friendship with God.

Personal Notes

Personal Notes

The "Bite Sized Bible Study Series"
By Beth Jones

When your words came, I ate them;
they were my joy and my heart's delight . . .
Jeremiah 15:16 NIV

- Six practical Bible studies for Christians living in today's culture.
- Each book contains 6 sessions designed for individual & small group study.
- Great studies targeting men, women, believers and seekers of all ages.
- Convenient size 6" x 9", each book is between 80-144 pages.
- Fill-in-the-blank book with Group Discussion questions after each session.
- "Nuggets" throughout each study explain Scriptures in easy to follow way.
- Written in a contemporary style using practical illustrations.
- Perfect for small group curriculum, bookstores and churches.

Satisfied Lives For Desperate Housewives
God's Word On Proverbs 31
Great Study For Women, Retail $7.99
ISBN: 1-933433-04-3

Session 1: Desperate For God
Session 2: Desperate For Balance
Session 3: Desperate For A Great Marriage
Session 4: Desperate For Godly Kids
Session 5: Desperate To Serve
Session 6: Desperate For Purpose

Grace For The Pace
God's Word For Stressed & Overloaded Lives
Great Study For Men & Women, Retail $7.99
ISBN: 1-933433-02-7

Session 1: Escape From Hamsterville
Session 2: Help Is Here
Session 3: How Do You Spell Relief?
Session 4: Get A Bigger Frying Pan
Session 5: Houston, We Have A Problem!
Session 6: Time Keeps On Ticking

Call Or Go Online To Order:
800-596-0379
www.valleypresspublishers.com

Kissed Or Dissed
God's Word For
Feeling Rejected & Overlooked
6 SESSIONS

BETH JONES

Kissed Or Dissed

God's Word For Feeling Rejected & Overlooked
Great Study For Women, Retail $7.99
ISBN: 1-933433-01-9

Session 1: Dissed 101
Session 2: Blessed & Highly Favored
Session 3: Edit Your Life
Session 4: That's What I'm Talking About
Session 5: Sow Acceptance Seeds
Session 6: Just Like Jesus

What To Do When
You Feel Blue
God's Word For
Depression & Discouragement
6 SESSIONS

BETH JONES

What To Do When You Feel Blue

God's Word For Depression & Discouragement
Great Study For Men & Women, Retail $7.99
ISBN: 1-933433-00-0

Session 1: When The Sky Is Not Blue
Session 2: No Pity Parties Allowed
Session 3: The Things You Could Think
Session 4: Go To Your Happy Place
Session 5: You've Got To Have Friends
Session 6: Lift Up The Down

The Friends
God Sends
God's Word On
Friendship & Chick Chat
6 SESSIONS

BETH JONES

The Friends God Sends

God's Word On Friendship & Chick Chat
Great Study For Women, Retail $7.99
ISBN: 1-933433-05-1

Session 1: Friendship Realities
Session 2: The Friendship Workout
Session 3: God-Knit Friendships
Session 4: Who's On Your Boat?
Session 5: Anatomy of A Friendship Famine
Session 6: A Friend of God

Don't Factor
Fear Here
God's Word For Overcoming
Anxiety, Fear & Phobias
6 SESSIONS

BETH JONES

Don't Factor Fear Here

God's Word For Overcoming Anxiety, Fear & Phobias
Great Study For Men & Women, Retail $7.99
ISBN: 1-933433-03-5

Session 1: Fear of Death
Session 2: Fear of Man
Session 3: Fear of Danger
Session 4: Fear of Change
Session 5: Fear Factors - Peace & Love
Session 6: Fear Factors - Faith & Courage

BethJones.org

a
simple
casual
blog

articles
and
bible
studies

topics
like
eternal life
girl stuff
healing
ministry
finances
holy spirit
prayer
victory
faq

click
it

.